Woven on the Loom of Time

Many Faiths and One Divine Purpose

M. Darrol Bryant

Decent Books

New Delhi

Published and Printed by
Decent Books
'Suryodaya'
D-36/A-1, Mohan Garden
Najafgarh Road
New Delhi - 110 059

Distributed by
D.K. Printworld (P) Ltd.
Regd. office
'Sri Kunj', F-52, Bali Nagar
New Delhi - 110015
Phones : (011) 545-3975, 546-6019; *Fax* : (011) 546-5926
E-mail: dkprint@4mis.com

ISBN 81-86921-06-0

First published in 1999

Contents

1

Opening the Subject

. . . the various religious systems that exist and prevail in this world today are ever so many ways of approaching the one Supreme Cosmic Reality, which is transcendental and cannot be encompassed . . . all religions have come into existence in global human society . . . in order to bring humanity back to the eternal source of being.[1]

I AM deeply honoured to have been invited by Professor T.S. Devadoss, Head of the Radhakrishnan Institute for Advanced Study of Philosophy, on behalf of the University of Madras, to give the 1994 Principal Miller Endowment Lectures. That honour has two aspects. First, I am pleased to be included in the company of those distinguished Indian scholars who have given these lectures in the past.[2] Second, I am honoured to have been invited to address a topic of such magnitude.

The topic of the Principal Miller Lectures here at the University of Madras is large and, in some respects, forbidding. Let me explain. The topic was intially given to me — or at least I so understood it — in two different forms. First, I understood that I was to address the topic of "God's one developing purpose in history." Then it was later clarified that the precise formulation of the topic was "the inner meaning of human history as disclosing

1. Swami Chidananda, *IRFWP Newsletter* I/2, 1993, pp. 13-14.
2. See the special edition of the *Journal of Philosophy*, University of Madras, 1990.

the one increasing purpose that runs through the ages." Either formulation is troubling. Why? The formulation reflects a time and a world that, in the contemporary West, has largely passed. While these formulations made sense within the context of Principal Miller's own Calvinist-Christian and Presbyterian world that shared a conviction of 'divine overarching purpose' and of the 'divine disposal of history' towards those ends, these are not convictions easily assumed in the post-modern Western world. The modern era substituted the idea of 'progress' fueled by modern science and technology and coupled with imperial political power for the notion of 'purpose.' And post-modern 'deconstructing' Western intellectuals would have us believe that there is no such thing as purpose at all.[3]

Even in Principal Miller's time, these convictions were not universally or unambiguously held even by those within the Calvinist-Presbyterian world, or within the larger Christian world. This does not necessarily mean that they are not true but only that the world they assumed and the mode of discourse in which they were articulated were not shared by all. Nor could these Calvinist-Christian assumptions be assumed to be universally held convictions, though there were comparable convictions to be found in different traditions. However, these

---

3. While many in our post-modern world would reject Miller's conviction of 'overarching purpose' and 'divine disposal of history,' I do acknowledge the truth to which these formulations point. My point, however, is that we must be aware that this discourse is not shared by all.

The 'post-modern' philosophy of 'deconstruction' is too large a subject to address here. Nor does it merit a long discussion, but it is symptomatic of the state of Western intellectual life. For my brief effort to address some of those issues, see "From 'De' to 'Re' or . . . Does the 'Future of Ontotheology' Require the Recovery of the Experience/Sense of Transcendence?" In Henry Ruf (ed.), *Religion, Ontotheology, and Deconstruction*, New York: Paragon Press, 1989, pp. 69-87.

misgivings have been largely overcome due to some fortuitous events that occurred upon my arrival here in Madras.

The day after I arrived in Madras, I was a guest in Professor Devadoss' home. His father T. Sundarabalu, a remarkable man then in his nineties, was part of our conversation when I asked about Principal Miller. Mr. Sundarabalu enthusiastically joined the conversation, as he had studied at Madras Christian College and had met Principal Miller. He then went to his room and returned with a slim volume on Principal Miller that had been published in the 1920s. In that volume I discovered that Principal Miller had been deeply concerned about the very questions I wished to address in these lectures — the many faiths and the one purpose — and that he had been remarkably open to the other traditions of faith and life. Indeed, Miller had already anticipated some of the positions I have sought to present here. Thus I felt relieved that I would be pursuing an exploration that was both in the spirit and purview of the one for whom this lecture series was founded.[4]

None the less, I was somewhat surprised when reading the contributions of earlier holders of this lectureship. What surprised me was that there were virtually no reservations about addressing this topic, nor seldom any recognition of the particular context that had shaped the very formulation of the topic.[5] Rather, it

4. The volume was entitled **Dr. William Miller**, and was written in the mid-1920s. In it there is a chapter on the "Christian Conception of God's Dealings with Mankind" where we read that "God's compassion was working on and in and among all men. Mankind was a unity" (47), that "it was not true that the Christian church had a monopoly of divine truth" (49), and that "the same God had been guiding and inspiring all the nations of the earth and that in no age or nation did God leave Himself without witness." (49) I was delighted with this discovery since it reassured me that my topic was appropriate for the Principal Miller Lectures.

5. The notable exception was the essay by T.M.P. Mahadevan cited below.

seemed that the several philosophers, many committed to Vedānta, took up the topic as their own, assuming that we all shared a common discourse and common assumptions about the nature of things. I must admit that I do not believe that we can now proceed as if there is a commonly held universe of discourse, or a common world-view. Rather, it has become necessary in philosophical and religious reflection to be aware, so far as possible, of the cultural and religious contexts which shape one's discourse and provide the assumptions for one's reflection. It is only in the light of such awareness that we can attempt to speak cross-culturally and inter-religiously — as we must if we are to adequately address the topic of the Miller Lectures.[6]

---

6. Let me illustrate this problem of discourse and our assumed contexts with one example, one central to what I will be attempting to do here. As you will discover, 'religion' is central to the perspective that I will attempt to articulate in these lectures. But is this the term that I should use for saying what I wish to say? Is it a word that is adequate to the variety and reality of humankind's religious Ways? The term 'religion' has emerged relatively recently in the English language. Its semantic origins seem to be the Latin term 'religare,' meaning 'to bind together.' Yet in English the term religion has come to mean, for many, essentially Christianity and a belief in a personal Supreme Diety. But how is this meaning adequate to what the Hindus call *dharma* and the Muslims call *dīn*? The problem is compounded since the Sanskrit term *dharma* is not equivalent to the Arabic word *dīn*. (See the discussion of *dīn* in S. Murata and W. C. Chittick, *The Vision of Islam*, New York: Paragon Press, 1994, pp. xxx-xxxv.) And both of these terms are richer than the English word 'religion.' Yet *dharma* and *dīn* are often translated into English as equivalents to the English word 'religion.' Further, each term takes on distinctive meanings and associations within the context of the respective traditions in which they occur: the Hindu and the Muslim. It is further complicated by the fact that *dharma* (Pali, *dhamma*) is also used in the Buddhist context. The consequence of assuming that these are equivalents is that we not only fail to →

It is important to understand that in the modern Western world, we have experienced a profound assault on both of the convictions that are central to Principal Miller's concern: God and Purpose. Those assaults have come from several sources: modern Western academic philosophy, modern science or more accurately 'scientism,' from awareness of the multiplicity of cultures and the consequent 'relativism,' and even from theologians who have proclaimed 'the death of god.'[7] Though we

---

→ truly understand one another, but the heart of what each term is attempting to point to is lost.

Indeed, the problems in relation to the term 'religion' and its adequacy to what diverse traditions value so deeply and name in such diverse ways are so troubling that one prominent Western scholar, Wilfrid Cantwell Smith, has even suggested that we abandon the term altogether. (See W. C. Smith, *The Meaning and End of Religion, A New Approach to the Religious Traditions of Mankind*, New York: Macmillan, 1963) Likewise, W.C. Smith objects to terms like Hinduism, Buddhism, Christianity, etc., as abstractions that distort rather than communicate the reality of these, Smith's preferred term, 'faiths.' This proposal is not accepted here, but I remain troubled concerning the word that I should use to convey what is intended, namely, the living reality of the Ways to the Ultimate.

If I were simply to assume the universality of my discourse, then it would carry many associations and meanings that are not adequate in the discourse of another tradition. Nor even in this case, to my own purposes. Consequently, although I will often use the term 'religion'—and sometimes 'Way' and rarely *dharma* — I hope it will be heard as a pointer word and that the reader will also recall some of those larger and richer senses that are conveyed by terms like *dharma* and *dīn*.

7. A complete bibliography on all the topics catalogued here is neither possible nor particularly helpful, but I would like to especially mention the critique of 'scientism' found in Huston Smith, *Forgotten Truth, The Common Vision of the World's Religions*, New York: Harper Collins, 1976, esp. pp. 1-18.

will not address these issues here, we must at least acknowledge them, for they provide part of the background to my attempt to address the theme of the Miller lectures. Moreover, when one turns to recent works of history, one finds little that can help us address this question. Again, Western historiography has largely eschewed the question of purpose and certainly looks with suspicion on any claim that the historical process discloses any purposes other than those of power-seeking human beings, and certainly not ultimate ones.[8]

In the face of recent developments, especially in the Western history of thought, it might be prudent to be silent in the face of

8. A singular exception was Eugen Rosenstock-Huessy (1888-1973) whose work did not influence contemporary academic historiography, but always moved and inspired me. Indeed, I am indebted to him in innumerable ways, as these lectures make clear. Thus the clues to this performance are the works of Eugen Rosenstock-Huessy and more than thirty years of listening to the religious traditions of humankind in the encounter and dialogue between religions or the divine *līlā* of the interplay of traditions in a post-modern world. Ever since I walked the prairie landscape of North Dakota under a boundless sky and land and met the native or first-peoples along with my own Christian Way, I have had a sense that one can only understand if one opens oneself, stands under and listens, receives what is given to one. This sense grew as I read in college Huston Smith's *Religions of Man*, New York: Harper & Row, 1958 (since revised and republished as *The World's Religons, Our Great Wisdom Traditions*, San Francisco: HarperSanFrancisco, 1991) and Mircea Eliade's *Sacred and Profane*, New York: Harper & Row, 1961, two books that made a deep impression on me. As I learned of the many ways to the Ultimate, I was not tempted to a simple relativism but awoke to a conviction that one must attempt to hear the chord played in the midst of the seeming cacophany of the many religions and their seemingly contradictory claims. I came to believe that one might see, at least dimly, the vision that illumines the tumult of images that everywhere abound. These lectures are, →

the question of purposes in history. Such silence is perhaps doubly appropriate given the problematic I have set for myself, namely, to relate the question of 'the one developing purpose through the ages' to the many religious traditions of humankind. And, if, as I earlier suggested, we cannot simply assume a given religious or intellectual tradition, where are we to turn to address this question? My suggestion is — and the path I will follow here — that we turn to the religious traditions of humankind as a whole. When we look not only at a particular tradition, but at all the traditions, is there any shared conviction concerning the question of divine purposes in history? At one level, the answer is no. Each tradition speaks in its own terms, with its own mythology, its own convictions and beliefs: Hindus speak of Liberation, Buddhists of Enlightenment, and Christians of the Kingdom of God. Some traditions, for example, the Hindu, are more cosmic in their orientation, and some, for example, the Jewish, more historical. Even 'history' is understood differently, as some traditions emphasise its masking of the Real, while others see history as the Real.

None the less, there is, I will argue here, a surprising unanimity at another level. There emerges across the religious traditions a remarkable unanimity on the purpose of history, one that cuts across the cosmic/historical and *māyā*/history divide. We find in the religious tradition a shared conviction that the deepest purpose of life in time is the encounter with the Ultimate. Of course, that unanimity is articulated in the diverse discourses, symbols and world-views of those traditions. That great unanimity can perhaps be formulated as a series of interlocking affirmations. But before offering an anticipatory

---

→ in a sense, my report after years of listening. At times, it is given to me with an intuitive clarity and certainty that floods my heart with joy and my mind with light; at others, it retires and leaves me inwardly uncertain and confused. I fear that this attempt moves within those ambiguities as well.

account of those affirmations, I must make clear the operating assumptions, at least those of which I am aware, in these lectures.

II

SEVEN ASSUMPTIONS AND DISTINCTIONS

First, I have turned to the religious life of humankind in search of a way to address the question of purpose and meaning in history. My assumption is that it is within the multiform history of religion that one will find the wisdom that can give us orientation towards our question. This is an assumption at odds with modern Western historical writing, which tells the story of the human journey in time largely in terms of political, social and economic forces. For example, Marxian historians see the central dynamic of history as the conflict between the owners of the means of production and the workers, the economic force. Everything else is considered superstructural, or a mere reflection of these deeper economic realities. Liberal historians see history as the march towards liberal, democratic, political and social institutions. Religion figures in such histories but only as part of the social trends that are considered fundamental to the social process. In this lecture, I assume that the story of human unfolding is centered in the spiritual life, and that our most profound clues to the life of the spirit are found in the religious traditions of humankind.

However, I am not claiming, as seems often to be the case in modern historical studies, that all of history is to be reduced to a particular dimension or aspect of that vast story, in this case religion. Rather, I am simply announcing where I have turned in order to gain the resources required to address the question of 'purposes and inner meanings.' The very formulation of the topic and its emphasis on 'inner meanings' and 'purpose' — the specific phrase 'one developing purpose through the ages' comes from Lord Tennyson's poem, "Locksley Hall"[9] — makes clear

9. See Tennyson's Locksley Hall in the *Collected Works*.

that we cannot simply discern meaning by a recitation of the outer events of history. Nor, on the other hand, can we simply ignore historical realities in addressing the question. Both of these options we will seek to avoid.

In turning to the religious traditions, I share a conviction that is evident in the other Miller lectures, namely, that philosophy is not separate from religion. Rather, philosophy as the love or friend (philia) of wisdom (sophia), shares with religion/*dharma* the quest for the truth of things. This conviction was long part of the Western traditions as well, but in the modern era we have encountered a great divorce between things philosophical and things religious that has left philosophy the poorer. Western academic philosophy largely ignores, if it is not overtly hostile to, religion.

Secondly, I am persuaded that it is no longer adequate to address this issue simply by appealing to a single religious tradition, even though one tradition rather than another may play a larger role in one's vision and thinking. While the religious traditions have provided us with the mythic narratives that address the questions of purpose and meaning, each tradition has often assumed a universality for its mode of discourse — an assumption that is unwarranted. The meeting of traditions — what I have elsewhere called 'the divine *līlā* of interreligious encounter and dialogue'[10] — is creating a new context for the question. The context is, as Wilfred Cantwell Smith has recently argued, the history of religion as a whole.[11] For Smith — and I am in agreement with this part of his thesis — history, especially

---

10. The title of an unpublished paper I delivered at the University of Victoria in 1992.

11. See Wilfred Cantwell Smith, *Towards a World Theology*, Philadelphia: Westminster, 1981, especially pp. 3-20 entitled "A History of Religion in the Singular." Smith argues that "the history of men and women's religious life . . . is intrinsically the locus of both the mundane and the transcendent." (3)

the history of religion, is, in large measure, the story of the encounter with Transcendence.

While the history of religion as a whole — or in the singular — provides the context for these reflections, I cannot pretend to have a position outside that history, nor to have knowledge of all traditions, nor to have grasped that whole history. Rather, I have come to consciousness in the context of the Christian aspect of that story and have been shaped by its wisdom and the self-disclosure/revelation of God given in that tradition. I attempt to stand deliberately within that tradition while at the same time seeking to understand and learn from the other great streams of religious life. Consequently, my language, as well as my outlook has been shaped by the Christian tradition. But it has also been shaped by more than thirty years of study of the religious life of humankind. While I initially focused on the Christian tradition, I have been for fifteen years deeply involved in interreligious encounter and dialogue. Thus my awareness of the other great traditions has grown through contact with believers/practitioners in those traditions, through participation in their religious life and practice, and through reading the literature from the different traditions, their sacred scriptures and expositors. This is part of my own attempt to grasp the meaning of the remarkable story of human religious life in its encounter with Transcendence.[12]

Thirdly, I approach the question in the context of the human religious quest for meaning and orientation within the dialectic of time and eternity. Although the post-modern era rejects the premise of the Transcendent and argues that the quest for meaning can be adequately addressed within the context of a universe that exists from itself alone, those are assumptions

12. That story begins in my childhood on the prairies of North Dakota under a boundless sky that provided me with my first sense of God Beyond, an awareness and icon of that Ultimate Mystery that ever exceeds our grasp.

from which I (and, for that matter, the vast majority of men and women now living on this planet) dissent. Moreover, the subsequent experience of modern Western humanity — its anomie, meaninglessness, and alienation — makes that a dubious assumption.

Fourthly, I understand one essential clue to our question to lie in the mythic narratives to be found in the religious life of humankind. These mythic narratives address the quest for meaning and orientation in terms of the stories of the Ultimate and the Human. Mircea Eliade, the great historian of religion, called them 'the stories of the gods.' Northrup Frye, a great Canadian literary critic, called these narratives 'encyclopedic myths.'[13] The Christian Scriptures, for example, unfold the human journey from creation to consummation. The great Indian epic, the *Mahābārata*, which contains the *Bhagavad Gītā*, 'opens the eyes of the world blinded by ignorance.' They do not address the narrow questions of what happened and when — the central questions of academic history — but rather the questions of the meaning of time and the human journey, the purposes of life, and the inner or spiritual meaning of human striving. Comparative and historical studies of religion show us that such mythic narratives are to be found in all religious traditions, even in the Buddhist, which does not affirm an understanding of the Transcendent as God.[14]

Such mythic narratives are not to be confused with what the Germans call 'historie,' or what English-speaking people call

---

13. See Mircea Eliade, *Patterns in Comparative Religion*, *op.cit.*, and Northrup Frye, *Anatomy of Criticism: Four Essays*, New York: Atheneum, 1957.

14. See, for example, Nirmal C. Sinha, *An Introduction to the History and Religion of Tibet*, Calcutta: Ambica Charan Bose, 1975, where he shows how Tibetan history is told as receiving, preserving, and living the *dharma*. Sinha argues that the wisdom of Tibetan Buddhism was "that a believer was to strive →

'history,' as a simple sequence of events. Indeed, one of the problems that has done much to discredit mythic narratives is the historicising of mythic narratives. For example, when Christians argue that God created the world in 6006 BC, they are guilty of this kind of historicising of the mythic narrative. The consequence is a misplaced debate, confusing modern views of time and history that aim at something other than what is aimed at in mythic narratives. This problem has also emerged in India in the current tragedy of Ayodhyā, where some Hindus seek to move the birth of Rām from its proper place in the mythic narrative into the realm of history. The result is confusion, conflict, and death.[15]

Klaus Klostermaier in an earlier Miller Lecture makes the point that what we need to examine in pursuing the questions

---

→ for the Enlightenment of all beings and not just for his own Enlightenment or that of his friends. In this view, liberation from suffering must be universal. . . . A true believer, a Bodhisattva or a Buddha in the making, should realise that Nirvāṇa is indivisible and therefore he must share his piety with the handicapped fellow travelers in the quest for Enlightenment." (p. 13) This is an example of the way a mythic narrative orients the self towards the whole and discloses the purpose of life. See also Mircea Eliade, *Patterns in Comparative Religion*, New York: World Publishing/Meridian Books, 1963, especially his discussion of myth as 'exemplary history.'

15. See Jonah Blank, *Arrow of the Blue Skinned God*, Boston: Houghton Mifflin, 1992, especially pp. 6ff. which observes that there are many temples in Ayodhyā — and elsewhere — all announcing themselves as the birthplace of Rama, but now that birth of the eternal which is infinitely repeatable has been historicised with dreadful consequences. One of the few courageous Hindu leaders to speak out on this issue has been Dr. Shivamurthy Shivacharya of Sirigere in Karnataka; see his little volume *Communal Conflicts in India*, Sirigere: Sri Taralabalu Jagadguru Brihanmath, 1993, which contains his addresses to the Third Assembly of the World's Religions in

of the inner meaning and purpose of history is, in Indian terms, '*āgama*.' He describes '*āgama*' as ". . . comprehensive representations of insight into the meaning of the whole . . . ." And he continues.

> Traditional societies possess in their *āgamas* a storehouse of facts, patterns as well as meanings — overarched by an overall meaning from end to beginning, and the articulation of a purpose realised through history.[16]

His comments help to define what I am here calling mythic narratives. Klostermaier also points indirectly to the problem that now confronts us, namely, the erosion, if not loss, of those 'traditional societies' that shared these mythic narratives. Especially in the modern West, we have seen the emergence of a technological culture/society that is hostile to 'traditional societies', including the traditional christian societies of the West. There is no part of the world that is immune from these consequences. The technological way has become the new universal of our era.[17] And the consequence of this development is the erosion of mythic narratives, often replaced by more historicist narratives around national destiny, or technological

---

Seoul, Korea, in 1992, and his address to the Centenary Celebrations of the World Parliament of Religions in Bangalore in 1993. "The need of the hour is not to construct or demolish the masjid or mandir. Instead, we should aim at demolishing the walls of hatred and enmity in the minds of Hindus and Muslims and learn to live in harmony. . . .(p. 36) His is a courageous and important voice. It was also reported to me that Sai Baba said that 'the temple built in the heart to Ram' was the crucial matter, but I have not been able to confirm this.

16. Klaus Klostermaier, from the Miller Lecture *c*. 1981. The exact reference I have not been able to find due to the failure of a shipment of books to yet make their way back from India.

17. See M. Darrol Bryant, "Ecological Responsibility and Interfaith Dialogue," *Tibet House Newsletter*, Vol. 8 & 9, 1993-4, pp. 1-5.

progress, or a new age of englightenment and science.

Some, like the remarkable American ecologist Thomas Berry, have called for 'a New Story' that can incorporate the world given to us by the modern, natural sciences; but as sympathetic as I am to his critique of the technological era and the loss of an adequate 'cosmology,' I am less sanguine about the possibility of constructing new 'mythic narratives.'[18] The main reason is that they are not constructions but eruptions from the depths of the collective unconscious or revelations from the heights of the Beyond. Whatever their source, we may be better served by looking at what has been given to us in the great traditions and praying for their revitalisation rather than expecting someone to articulate 'a New Story.' It is precisely this revitalisation of traditions which is occurring in the contemporary encounter and dialogue of religions.

Fifth, I assume that the primary purpose of a mythic narrative is to provide orientation to our life in time as a whole. This is a necessity for the human spirit. Without orientation, we wander in confusion; with orientation, we gain direction and meaning. This religious meaning of a mythic narrative is its essential significance. It is not to be confused with the aims of the academic historian. The reason that human beings are moved by mythic narratives is not their isomorphic conformity to historical patterns or events, but because the human spirit requires orientation. Thus the truth of a mythic narrative lies in its existential and spiritual purpose: to render our life in time full of meaning because we have orientation towards the whole.

---

18. See Thomas Berry, *The Dream of the Earth*, San Francisco: Sierra Club, 1990 and A. Lonergan and Caroline Richards, (eds.), *Thomas Berry and the New Cosmology*, Mystic, CN: Twenty-Third Publications, 1988. Paul Tillich's comment about symbols, namely, that they 'live and die' is also relevant to issues of 'mythic narratives.' *Theology of Culture*, New York: Oxford University Press, 1964, pp. 53ff.

Even where the mythic narratives found in the religious traditions have been explicitly rejected, they have been replaced by alternative stories (e.g., secular, technological or national ones) that function in a similar way.[19]

Sixth, it is necessary to clarify the term 'destiny' as it is central to the overall direction of these lectures. The noted Christian theologian Paul Tillich argued that human life unfolded within what he called 'ontological polarities.' These were three polar structures of life that he named as 'freedom and destiny,' 'dynamics and form,' and 'individuation and participation.'[20] 'Destiny' he defined as those dimensions of life given in biology, historical context and social setting. But this understanding of destiny does not lead to determinism since destiny unfolds in relation to human freedom. Nor is that freedom absolute, for it must actualise itself in the context of what is given in destiny. Likewise, dynamics and form also exist in a polar relationship. Without the dynamic element, we would end up in a sterile formalism; without the pole of form, there would be chaos. Likewise, the person is both part of a larger humanity in which one participates as well as a personal centre of consciousness. In these lectures, I attempt to walk this middle path, both affirming the destiny given to human unfolding in the pathways to the Ultimate yet acknowledging that that destiny is actualised in the freedom of humanity to participate in its own making. In one sense, this is Tillich's solution to the old, often misplaced debate, of freedom and determinism in Western thought. This issue,

---

19. See Mircea Eliade, *Myth and Reality*, New York: Harper and Row, 1963, especially pp. 162 ff. Eliade observes that "myths are the most general and effective means of awakening and maintaining consciousness of another world, a beyond, whether it be the divine world or the world of the Ancestors," p. 139.
20. See Paul Tillich, *Systematic Theology*, Vol. I, Chicago: University of Chicago Press, 1951, pp. 174-85, and also his *Courage to Be*, New Haven: Yale University Press, 1952.

which Tillich resolves in his doctrine of ontological polarities, has its counterpart in the debates concerning *karma* and freedom in Eastern traditions. The point here is that destiny should not be understood in mechanical or deterministic terms, but as that horizon which stands over the whole of the human journey in time and which is realised in the human journey towards the Ultimate.[21]

Finally, I want to clarify the way in which I am using the terms 'purpose,' 'purposes,' and 'ultimate purpose.' In the writings of Jonathan Edwards (1703-58), an eighteenth-century Puritan Christian theologian, we find some distinctions helpful for this exploration. In his treatise on *God's End in Creation*, Edwards argues that there are multiple ultimate ends in creation.[22] And among those ultimate ends we can distinguish what he called the 'chief ultimate end.' In Edwards vocabulary, this chief ultimate end is 'God's own glory.' And all things both participate in and contribute to that 'glory.' For Edwards, creation must have an end adequate to its beginning. Thus it is not possible, Edwards argued, since the beginning has its ground in that which exceeds it to find an end to creation within the context of creation itself. The End, like the Beginning, must be both present to creation and history yet exceed both. For Edwards, the name for the 'chief ultimate end' of creation was God's own

21. It is clear that human beings share at least one common end or destiny: death. But even here the religious traditions disclose their unity and diversity. The unity is their common conviction that the meaning of such an event, one common to all, means more than simply the end of biological life. Even death is to be understood as an encounter with something **more**, whether the consequences of one's *karma*, or the day of judgment, or acceptance into the loving light of God.

22. See Jonathan Edwards, *Dissertation Concerning the End For Which God Created the World, Works of President Edwards* (rpt. of Worcester edn., New York: Robert Carter and Bros., 1881) II, pp. 193ff.

glory. Human life is to reflect and participate in that end by way of the trinity — parallel to the *sat-cid-ānanda* formula of Hinduism — of being, knowledge, and joy. God created the universe in order to manifest divine glory and, according to Edwards, the purpose of creation is the communion of the Creator with the Creation. As the beginning of creation is communion of the Creator with the Creator's creation, so the end of creation is the creation's fulfilment in the Creator. Thus, for Edwards, the process of creation and history is one of realising God's Glory. Our gloss on his view and distinctions is that that glory is manifest in the making of humanity. We go beyond Edwards in seeing that making not only, as in Edwards, in relation to the 'work of redemption' which he sees in the unfolding of the Christian Way, but also in relation to the other classical traditions of religious life which are part of the making of humanity.[23] In this way, we seek to overcome an unexamined 'Christianity-centeredness' that too often informs the exploration of our subject.

Thus we can clarify the two-fold sense of the term 'purpose' as we are using the term here. Purpose means both the end or goal of an action or process, and the meaning of an act or process. Thus we ask 'why did you do that?' as well as 'what are you up

23. See M. Darrol Bryant, *Jonathan Edwards' Grammar of Time, Self, and Society*, Lewiston, NY: Edwin Mellen Press, 1993, esp. pp. 98ff. I do move beyond Edwards in this exploration. While Edwards saw the creation as universal, he restricted the work of redemption to the Christian story. (See Jonathan Edwards, *The History of Redemption*, Grand Rapids, MI: Associated Publishers & Authors, n.d., rpt. of 1773 edn. Originally given as a series of sermons in 1739, Edwards had intended to turn to them to create a work in 'a new method,' but death intervened.) But here I argue that the re-making of humanity is unfolded across the traditions of religious life as they participate in the making and remaking of humanity in the light of what is given in their dialogue with the Ultimate.

to?' 'what are your attempting?' 'what are you aiming at?' The question then is both one of end and meaning in relation to the whole of history.

In the light of the assumptions and the distinctions articulated above, I want to state, in a preliminary way, the interlocking affirmations that it will be the burden of these lectures to unfold.

III

FOUR AFFIRMATIONS

The first affirmation is that **the purpose of humanity is to be related to the Ultimate**. Within the religious traditions, this purpose is affirmed in the discourse that is particular to each tradition. In the Hindu traditions, for example, purpose is often expressed as attaining to the wisdom that *ātman* is *Brahman*, a wisdom so profound that it shatters the cycle of rebirth and results in liberation or *mokṣa*. In the Buddhist traditions, it is often articulated as the experience of Enlightenment, an insight so profound as to overcome suffering and achieve *nirvāṇa*. And some Mahāyāna traditions of Buddhism affirm that that purpose is not attained until all are Enlightened. In the Christian tradition, it is the conviction that life's purpose is communion with God, a purpose that restores humanity to its fullness. In Islam, it is expressed as the perfect peace that comes with surrender to Allāh wherein humanity achieves its full dignity. In Confucianism, purpose is seen as the harmony that arises from the cultivation of human-heartedness and the appropriate relationships with one another and Heaven's Mandate. Rather than seeing these as competing answers to the question of life's meaning and purpose, we can see them as parallel revelations of the whole, found in the diverse traditions of the religious life of humankind, that simultaneously give to and open up for humankind the spiritual orientation required to live life in relation to and in harmony with the Ultimate.[24]

In one sense, our first affirmation that the purpose of life is to be related to the Ultimate, is consistent with a doctrine of what Aldous Huxley called the 'perennial philosophy' or what Huston Smith called 'the primordial tradition.' That doctrine affirms a common end and purpose for humanity found in all religious traditions, namely, 'to identify' oneself with the "eternal Self and so come to unitive knowledge of the Divine Ground."[25] Though I would qualify the use of the language of a particular Hindu tradition to make this affirmation — as I have attempted to do with my own Christian discourse — I am generally in agreement with the intention. But I think it is imperative to take seriously the plurality of revelations of the Ultimate and the particularity of the historical unfolding of the different pathways. It is especially this latter point that I am attempting to make in arguing for the historical role of the traditions in the distinctive ways that they have related human life to the Ultimate.

The second affirmation is that **history is the spiritual story of human unfolding in time**. And it is already **in time** — on the loom of time — that the relationship to the Ultimate is being unfolded. And central to that unfolding is the religious life of humankind, the many paths by which this divine/spiritual purpose is achieved. Religions are the meeting place of the human and the divine. The particular ways given in the great traditions are the matrices for the nurture of particular divine-human types: for the Buddhists to realise our Buddhahood, for the Hindu to realise *ātman*, for the Muslim to perfectly submit to Allāh as exemplified in the prophet Muhammad, for the

24. See Leonard Swidler (ed.), *Toward a Universal Theology of Religion*, Maryknoll, NY: Orbis Books, 1987. It includes contributions from Buddhist, Hindu, Muslim, and Taoist traditions.

25. *Bhagavad Gītā*, New York: Mentor Classics, 1951, Aldous Huxley, 'Introduction,' p. 13.

Christian to become Christlike, for the Sikh to become a disciple of the Divine *guru*, for the Confucian to live the five great relationships in harmony, for the Taoist to live in the rhythm of the Tao. Each of these pathways of the spirit has its own integrity and distinctness in relation to that which is Transcendent or Beyond, a Beyond that exceeds all our reckoning.[26]

The temptation of every religion is to hear what is given to it in its originating — and overwhelming — experience of the Absolute/Divine/God as exhaustive of the Ultimate. But here it is crucial to distinguish between complete or full experiences of the Ultimate and exhaustive experiences of the Ultimate. The Ultimate is, from the human side, inexhaustible; it is in itself utterly beyond all categories, ineffable. On the other hand, the religious form must house the Spirit and give us a Way to the Ultimate. A similar point can be made in relation to those traditions which have a revealed Scripture. Again, no scripture is exhaustive of the Absolute. However, this does not mean that any scripture should not be regarded as the Revelation of the Absolute. Every revealed Scripture may be sufficient to exhaust our minds and comprehension, but never to exhaust the reality of the One Beyond. This distinction is parallel to the exoteric/esoteric distinction but with this difference: while the esoteric mind is able to understand and affirm the exoteric vision, the reverse is not true. Thus this esoteric reading of the religions will not be acceptable to the exoteric mind.

The third affirmation is that the spiritual process that lies

---

26. See Donald W. Mitchell, *Spirituality and Emptiness, The Dynamics of Spiritual Life in Buddhism and Christianity*, New York: Paulist Press, 1991, especially pp. 10 ff. for a discussion of emptiness and 'absolute nothingness.' Some Buddhist traditions are more open to discussions of the Ultimate then others. See Robert Carter (ed.), *God, The Self, and Nothingness*, New York: Paragon House, 1990.

at the inner heart of history is **the 'making of humanity,' the fitting of humanity for communion with the divine**. That making is the mystery[27] that lies at the heart of the many religious pathways, their practices, their rituals, their disciplines, their beliefs, and their values. It is through these constellations of practices, beliefs, rituals, and values that humanity becomes what it becomes as it practices, believes, performs, values. The paradox of each religion is that we are not what we truly are. We must awaken to that Buddhahood that we already are, we must realise the *ātman* that we already are, we must become the sons and daughters of God in whose image we were made, and so on and so forth. The different religious traditions account in diverse ways for this paradoxical need to become what we most profoundly are. The fact that we are not what we are is due to ignorance, *tanha*, sin, grasping, attachments, forgetfulness. But each religious pathway creates its own distinctive Way to that end of overcoming and becoming what we truly are. And, in the process, each calls into being a form of humanity that we name in the languages of the different traditions as Buddhist, Christian, Hindu, Muslim, Sikh, Taoist, Confucian, etc.[28] And the differences

---

27. The term 'mystery' needs to be clarified. It is not to be confused with the term 'mystify' meaning to obscure. It is meant in its classical Christian sense, namely, as 'exceeding our capacity to exhaust,' not 'exceeding our capacity to know.' In the early Christian christological debates, it was the term used to speak about the 'divine and human in Christ.' It is properly speaking a 'mystery,' since even though we believe that Christ is fully God and fully human, we cannot fully grasp nor fully explain the relationship of the divine and the human in Christ; hence it is a mystery. Here when we use the term mystery we are pointing to the 'more' that always exceeds our categories and understandings.

28. The often repeated claim that 'all religions are the same' is not one that I share. Such a notion reduces the manifest multiformity of religious life to mere appearance and betrays the historic role of the different traditions as different Ways to →

between these forms of humanity in relation to the Ultimate are not necessarily contradictory. They are simply the names of our multiform humanity in the making of that humanity in relation to the Ultimate.

→ the Ultimate. To acknowledge their differences is not to counsel conflict, but to plead for respect for the integrity of the diverse ways and to seek their unity not at the level of their historic actuality, but in relation to their aspiration towards the Beyond. Moreover, when one looks more closely at arguments for the sameness of religion, one discovers that the identity or sameness of religion is achieved by assimilating the diverse religious traditions into the perspectives and discourse of one's own tradition. For example, when one looks closely at Svāmī Vivekānanda's claim that 'all religions are the same,' it turns out that, in his view, the inner core of all religions is his own Vedāntic faith. The same can be said for the view of a Christian thinker like Karl Rahner who finds that the exemplary representatives of other faiths are really 'anonymous Christians." Similarly, when the Dalai Lama says that 'all religions aim at happiness' he is speaking from within his own Buddhist faith. The consequence is that the historic particularity of each pathway is sacrificed for the sake of an affirmed sameness of all religions. Part of the reason for this confusion is that we fail to distinguish the shared aim of all religions, namely, to link human life to the Ultimate, from the particular Ways unfolded in the given tradition to achieve that shared End.

Furthermore, I do not find helpful the analogous assumption that, as argued by the British philosopher of religion John Hick, that all religions are ways of salvation. Again, it is to impose on all religions the categories of one religion, in this case the Christian category of 'salvation.' (See John Hick, *An Interpretation of Religion, Human Responses to the Transcendent*, London: Macmillan, 1989.) This runs in the face of the diverse ways in which traditions understand the goal of their path: for Buddhists it is Enlightenment, not salvation; for the Hindu it is Liberation, not salvation; for the Muslim it is Submission, not salvation. While I agree with →

On the other hand, I do agree with the *Dhammapada* when it says, "Many do not know that we are here in this world to live in harmony. Those who do know this do not fight against each other."[29] And that harmony includes the harmony of the religious Ways of humankind. But harmony is not identity as singleness. Harmony rather acknowledges multiplicity and the particular while seeing that it is as all ways are lived that harmony is achieved. Taken together, the religious traditions sing a

---

→ Hick in affirming the authenticity of the many Ways to the Ultimate, it is not necessary to collapse those ends into a single category. Part of the problem with Hick's position is that he denies knowledge of the 'Real *an sich*,' rather than realising that the Absolute, the Ultimate, the Real, is given to us in the revelatory traditions, but not given absolutely or exhaustively.

I must also acknowledge my debt to the Unification movement, founded in 1954 in Seoul, Korea as the Holy Spirit Association for the Unification of World Christianity. In an effort to protect their civil rights and as a protest against the hysteria that often surrounded this, and other new religious movements, I have been in an on-going conversation with this controversial, but significant religious group since the late 1970s. Though I dissent from many of the views found in this movement, especially the claims concerning Rev. and Mrs. Sun Myung Moon, I must also admit that they have been an important stimulus to my own thinking about these matters. Moreover, I have been happily associated with many of the ecumenical and interreligious initiatives funded by the movement. These include the New Ecumenical Research Association (New ERA), the Assembly of the World's Religions (AWR), the Council for the World's Religions (CWR), the International Religious Foundation (IRF) and the Interreligious Federation for World Peace (IRFWP). The work sponsored by these institutions have always been shaped and directed by an interfaith group of non-Unificationists. This work has provided me with a remarkable opportunity for dialogue with people from virtually all the world's religious traditions.

29. *Dhammapada*, I.6.

harmonious whole that incorporates the particular notes without resolving them into a simple identical one. The musical metaphor is appropriate since it incorporates unity in diversity and also acknowledges that only with the many can the harmony be sounded.

Of course, the notion of the harmony of religious pathways has certainly not been foremost in the religious life of humankind. Recognising the harmony of *dharma* is, I believe, the spiritual challenge of our age. And I am further persuaded that one way to recognise and realise that inter-religious or cross-religious harmony is through interfaith dialogue. In this movement, the integrity of the particular traditions is respected while the things shared across tradition are also recognised. Mutual recognition and understanding is the aim rather than an eclectic spirituality or a new syncretism. When persons of different faiths meet, it is not for the sake of saying we are all the same, nor for the sake of the mutual transformation of what is essential to each Way. Rather it is for the sake of understanding each other and deepening appreciation of what is given in each tradition. The end of dialogue is the unity of polyphonic humankind. From encounter and dialogue can grow patterns of mutuality and a deepening of our respective traditions.[30]

The fourth affirmation is that we discover **the harmony of the diverse religious pathways not at the level of particular practices, disciplines, beliefs, rituals, and values** but in what Frithjof Schuoun calls their 'transcendent unity.'[31] Or, to use

---

30. See my *Religion in a New Key*, New Delhi: Wiley Eastern Ltd., 1992, especially pp. 35ff.

31. Frithjof Schuon, *The Transcendent Unity of Religions*, New York: Harper & Row, 1975. Compare with the position taken here Schuon's remarks in another essay, "No Activity Without Truth," that "the Absolute or the Infinite... is what gives sense to our existence, just as one must know that the essential content of life is the consciousness of this supreme reality, a →

another metaphor, we might say that the shared purpose of religion is to transport us to 'the further shore.'[32] But the boats to ferry us are not themselves the further shore. They are the diverse pathways of the spirit, pathways that remain distinct and exoteric within time. When we look at the particular practices, beliefs, rituals, and values of any given religious tradition, we first encounter difference. One believes this, another affirms that, one practices in this way, another in that, one enacts this ritual, another that. As one gets closer and deeper, one may become aware of similarities, analogies, parallels, and even, occasionally, commonalities across tradition. There are things shared, but difference remains none the less. Unity is not historical identity, nor is harmony sameness. Harmony emerges when the various ways are all seen together, and harmony can only be heard if our ears are attuned to their unity in the Transcendent. Thus we can only point to this harmony; we cannot demonstrate it, nor can it be adequately conceptualised. It is ineffable. It constantly exceeds us yet beckons us to hear its music.

The affirmations that (1) the purpose of humanity is to be related to the Ultimate, (2) that the spiritual quest is at the heart of history and that it is enfolded in the multiform traditions of spiritual life, (3) that the spiritual drama unfolding in history is the making of humanity through the diverse traditions, and (4) that the unity of the religious traditions is not phenomenal but transcendent are interlinked. Taken together, they constitute a way of understanding the religious life of humankind and a

---

→ fact that explains the part to be played by continual prayer; in a word, we live to realise the Absolute." (38) Earlier he had claimed that "the essence of revelation — or enlightenment — is one, but human nature requires diversity." (33) *The Sword of Gnosis*, comp. J. Needleman, Baltimore: Penguin, 1974.

32. Swami Abhishiktananda, *The Further Shore*, Delhi: ISPCK, 1975.

vision of meaning and purpose. A vision is not the same as a conceptual grid, nor is it a philosophical construct. Rather, it is an attempt to articulate an intuition of something that exceeds our grasp yet gives orientation towards the truth of what is. In this context, the vision I seek to acknowledge is one that will allow us to see the larger purpose that is present within the religious life of humankind, a purpose that is both mediated through the particular traditions and exceeds those particular ways because their end is the Ultimate itself.

IV

ANTICIPATING THE ARGUMENT

These affirmations and vision are, in brief, my answer to the question of the inner meaning of history and the one unfolding purpose. My proposal is that we see the inner meaning of history as the story of the unfolding quest for the Ultimate. That purpose is not to be reduced to the story of any particular religious Way. It is not to be seen in terms of a single tradition but in the plurality of historical religious forms that mediate the task of the making of humanity in relation to the Ultimate, the Beyond. Thus we discover that that one purpose is realised through the multiple pathways. While some have hinted at such a vision in the past, it is in the present, through interreligious encounter and dialogue, that we are beginning to awaken most profoundly to this shared end that is the 'one increasing purpose running through the ages.' That purpose was eloquently articulated in the beautiful image of T.M.P. Mahadevan, in an earlier Miller lecture, when he observes that 'in the great cosmic drama of Time', the 'purpose is to unveil the face of Eternity.'[33]

---

33. T.M.P. Mahadevan, *Journal of Philosophy*, p. 144. It is this vision that we have begun to glimpse in the contemporary dialogue of religions. However, some of the categories that have emerged in that discussion have obscured rather than clarified that purpose. Thus, I believe it is essential that we →

But how are we to see that unveiling in relation to the diverse religious traditions, all of which claim to point us to that very Eternity? Obviously, I do not believe we have to see this by choosing one religion and rejecting all the others, nor by absorbing all into one particular Way. But how are we then to see the multiform traditions in relation to that Eternal? Raimundo Panikkar in his book *Intra-Religious Dialogue* has made a valuable proposal, but it has not been widely taken up and explored. He suggests that rather than the inclusivist/exclusivist/pluralist alternatives that have dominated current thinking about the matter, we might consider another way. That other way is to see the multiform religious traditions in terms of what he calls 'parallelism.' He uses the image of the rainbow for this parallelist vision: each colour has its distinctive hue, but all together create the harmony which is the rainbow itself. Each of the colours of the rainbow refracts the light which is simultaneously beyond each particular hue yet fully present to each of the bands of colour. As beautiful as this image is, it is also limited. The limitation of this metaphor is its spatial context. We

---

→ move beyond such categories. There we often find three ways of characterising the relations between religions as exclusivism, inclusivism, and pluralism. Alan Race gave currency to these categories in his *Christians and Religious Pluralism*, London: SCM Press, 1983. Exclusivism is the attitude that sees truth in one's own religious tradition but denies that truth is present in other traditions. Inclusivism sees truth in other religious but articulates that truth in terms of one's own tradition. Pluralism is defined as an attitude that simply acknowledges the multiplicity of traditions but makes no attempt to see their unity. These categories are too much drawn from within the Christian traditions to be very helpful globally. And even within the Christian tradition, they have proved to be of only limited utility. We are suggesting that we move beyond these categories to a vision of the religions as religious pathways to the Ultimate, while still searching for adequate ways to express their shared ends and purposes.

need an image that can do justice simultaneously to the temporal dimension of religious life, and this, I suggest, is the utility of the metaphor of harmony. The image of the rainbow and the metaphor of harmony, taken together, may give us what we want.[34]

Or, it may simply be the case that we have not yet found adequate ways to express this shared, but multiform, quest for the Ultimate, nor a way to point to the harmony of *dharma*. My concern, one that has emerged in the context of the growing awareness of the multiplicity of religious pathways to the Ultimate in the history of religions and the living dialogue between religious traditions in the post-World War II world, is to develop a thesis concerning the place of the religious traditions in their common destiny: the Ultimate.

The argument is simple. I assume the unity of the human race and that it, on the basis of the witness of the world's religious traditions, has a common destiny: the Ultimate. In that context, then, I ask about the meaning of the different religious traditions. My answer is that they are means or crucibles for fitting humanity for the Ultimate, a process that unfolds in time and across time but is only fulfilled Beyond. But on the way to that conclusion I proceed through (a) an exposition of a philosophical anthropology that discloses humanity as constituted by Transcendence, (b) an analysis of the great religious traditions as the crucibles for the making of a multiform humanity in relation to the Ultimate, (c) an exposition of one Christian grammar of the spirit that attempts to see the process of making humanity in time, and (d) a summary conclusion. I include a poetic epilogue.

---

34. See Raimundo Panikkar, *The Intra-Religious Dialogue*, New York: Paulist Press, 1978.

2

Dialogical Humanity

In the Crucible of Transcendence

The Great Tao flows everywhere.
It may go left or right.
All things depend on it for life,
and it does not turn away from them.[1]

IN the first lecture, I sought to outline several of the assumptions that inform my exploration of the theme of the Principal Miller

1. *The Way of Lao Tzu*, tr. by Wing Tsit Chan, New York: Bobbs-Merrill, 1963, # 34, p. 160. I have deliberately selected a Taoist text to place at the head of this chapter in order to underscore the limitations of the term 'transcendence,' which I use here extensively. Transcendence is not meant as an equivalent to theistic as opposed to monistic, nor is it intended only to evoke notions of mere 'over-againstness' rather than 'deep withinness.' I had hoped the term might allow us to avoid the dualism of theism/non-theism. But my critics in Madras made me aware that the associations the term carried overran my hopes. So, let me say that my intent is to use the term 'transcendence' to point to that which is Ultimate, the Unconditioned, the Absolute, the Godhead, that which is beyond all of our divisions yet funds the whole, beyond the metaphors of 'over-against' and 'deep within' yet embracing those metaphors as part of the human experience of that which ever exceeds all our categories yet discloses itself and shines in those very experiences of the →

Lectures and sketched, in an anticipatory way, the elements of our argument concerning life's purpose and meaning in relation to the Ultimate. In this lecture, I will turn to a more contemporary philosophical argument that grounds humanity in the Ultimate. The same point could have been argued on the basis of the classical religious traditions — that we, in the language of theism, come from God and go to God, or, in the language of monism, that we are the Ultimate — but I have chosen this more contemporary route. It too seeks to ground our vision of humanity in the Ultimate and provides us with a vision of the religious traditions as a dialogue with Transcendence.

I

Let me begin by sketching the context within contemporary Western life that gave rise to the developments outlined below.

→ Ultimate which are at the centre of all. The use of the Taoist text is supported by Ellen Chen's comment that in # 34 and # 35 the "Tao is portrayed as the principle of plentitude." She goes on to characterise the Tao as 'like the Good of Plato,' yet even these characterisations are not exhaustive. (See Ellen Chen's fine translation *The Tao Te Ching*, New York: Paragon Press, 1989, p. 138.) My intention here also accords with that found in *The Divine Names* of Pseudo-Dionysius where we read that "with regard to the supra-essential being of God — transcendent Goodness transcendently there — no lover of the truth which is above all truth will seek to praise it as word or power or mind or life or being. No. It is at total remove from every condition, movement, life, imagination, conjecture, name, discourse, thought, conception, being, rest, dwelling, unity, limit, infinity, the totality of existence. And yet, since it is the underpinning of goodness, and by merely being there is the cause of everything, to praise this divinely beneficent Providence you must turn to all of creation. It is there at the centre of everything and everything has it for a destiny." (See *Pseudo-Dionysius, The Complete Works*, The Classics of Western Spirituality, tr. by Colm Luibheid, New York: Paulist Press, 1987, p. 54.)

Given the eclipse of Transcendence in Western intellectual life, it is not surprising that humanity has become a question to itself. Thus I want here to turn my attention to the perennial philosophical question of the nature of the human. It will be possible to adequately make a case for the religions only if we can, I believe, make the case for humanity as constituted by the Ultimate. Hence, in this lecture I want to argue, in a more philosophical idiom, for an understanding of the human as constituted by and unfolding in dialogue with Transcendence. This will be the first part of the argument for understanding the story of humankind as the encounter with the Ultimate and the centrality of the religious traditions in the making of humanity. In making this argument I will turn to the work of two figures, one Jewish, the other Christian, in the early twentieth century whose insights were partially forged in response to the challenges of modernity.

When modern existentialists spoke of the 'Geworfenheit' or 'thrownness' of humanity into the givens of historical time, they were prescient about the conditions of life in the twentieth century.[2] As we come to the end of this tumultuous century, humanity finds itself having endured a century of unprecedented change, unspeakable horror and unrelieved erosion of traditional patterns of meaning and life. The engine of unprecedented change has been the scientific and technological innovations that have altered humanity's relation to the earth and to itself. These changes have been Janus-faced, bringing both life and death in their wake. The unspeakable horror has been the

2. *Geworfenheit* is Martin Heidegger's term. See *Being and Time*, tr. by J. Macquarrie and E. Robinson, New York: Harper & Row, 1962, p. 174. Heidegger says that " 'thrownness' is meant to suggest the 'facticity of its being delivered over,' and goes on to characterize humanity as 'Dasein,' as finding 'itself in its thrownness.' " Here, the term is used to describe the human situation, but not strictly speaking in Heidegger's technical sense.

millions of lives obliterated in the mountains of Armenia, the ovens of Nazi Germany, the Gulags of the Soviet Union, the killing fields of Laos and Cambodia, and the snow-capped lands of Tibet.[3] Often we have seen how new technologies of destruction have been deployed in the name of purity and progress, creating lethal marriages of technology and ideology. And the erosion of traditional patterns of meaning and life have engulfed the planet in ways that leave no corner untouched. Hurled from their timeless life in the Kalihari Desert, the ! Kung or Bushman peoples of Southern Africa are no more immune from the erosion of traditional patterns than are the most sophisticated inhabitants of Manhattan, Paris, or Tokyo.[4]

While I do not believe that these events have altogether consumed older patterns of meaning, like those found in the

---

3. See Richard L. Rubenstein, *The Age of Triage: Fear and Hope in an Overcrowded World*, Boston: Beacon Press, 1983, for a disturbing and comprehensive account of this horror. For a profound grappling with the agony of the contemporary Jewish community, see Rubenstein's, *After Auschwitz: Radical Theology and Contemporary Judaism*, Indianapolis: Bobbs-Merrill, 1966, and, at a more personal level, see Richard Rubenstein, *Power Struggle*, New York: Charles Scribner's Sons, 1974. An earlier version of some of this material is included in a festschrift for Richard Rubenstein, *Reflections on the Thought of Richard Rubenstein: Triage, The Holocaust and Faith*, B. R. Rubenstein and M. Berenbaum (eds.), West Simsbury, Conn: Hedgehog Press, 1993, pp. 366-83. For a moving account of the tragedy of Tibet, see John Avedon, *In Exile from the Land of Snows*, New York: Vintage Books, 1986.

4. See Huston Smith, *Forgotten Truth: The Primordial Tradition*, New York: Harper & Row, 1973, for a penetrating analysis of modernity and its impact on our perception of the religious traditions of humankind. For a moving account of the Bushman peoples, see Laurens van der Post, *The Lost World of the Kalihari*, London: Penguin Books edition, 1962 and his *Heart of the Hunter*, London: Penguin edition, 1961.

great traditions of religious life, they do point to the challenge to speak the old wisdom in new idioms that dissent from the hubris of our age.

Within the 'thrownness' of our contemporary condition, some have discerned important new possibilities opened up to humanity. For example, the great Hindu philosopher S. Radhakrishnan (1888-1975), an Oxford Don, later President of India, and the one after whom this Institute for Advanced Studies in Philosophy is named, has remarked that the meeting of 'the peoples, races, cultures and religions' of the world is the phenomenon most 'characteristic of our times.'[5] It is, he continues, a meeting that in scope, scale, and potential significance has 'never before . . . taken place in the history of our world.'[6] This meeting has been made possible, ironically, by the very technologies that have also contributed to the erosion of traditional patterns of meaning and forms of life. The point of Radhakrishnan's observation, however, is neither the uniqueness of this historical moment — which has antecedents if not exact parallels — nor the ironies that have given rise to this situation. The crucial question is whether we will find in this encounter and meeting of peoples our way to a deepened and transformed awareness of humanity and its transcendent grounds. In Radhakrishnan's terms, the issue is whether or not the 'close neighbourhood' brought about by the conditions of modern life could be 'transformed into a true brotherhood,' whether or not 'the world' could become 'our home.'[7] For this hope to be well founded, it must have a basis and resonance within the very nature of our humanity and the reality of the human situation.

At the heart of our tumultuous era, then, lie fundamental philosophical issues that can easily be overlooked. These are the

---

5. S. Radhakrishnan, *Religion and Culture*, Delhi: Vision Books, 1968, rpt.1984, p. 51.
6. *Ibid.*
7. *Ibid.*

deeper matters that, often unrecognised, underlie discussions of economic or political issues, or discussions of modernisation or the transfer of technology or the challenge of democratisation. All of these processes point simultaneously to dimensions of the current crisis and to the struggle for the emergence of a planetary society, one founded on the awareness of our singular planet earth. Yet beneath these issues lie deeper philosophical matters that are provoked by these events. For we must also ask about the human beings and communities that find themselves caught up in these events. Thus the issue we will explore here is more obscure than these front page issues but equally significant. For at the inner heart of our emerging planetary society stands the question of the human itself. Who are we? What are we becoming? Can we rightly grasp the human except in relation to the Ultimate? What are the grounds that can sustain our quest for wholeness, community, and transcendence?

Early in this century, the question that humanity had become to itself led some European thinkers to a profound exploration of the dialogical foundations of humanity, a dialogue rooted in Transcendence. Their view of the life of humanity as dialogue provides a way into our thesis concerning the purpose and meaning of the human quest. It allows the religious pathways to come into view as integral to the divine dialogue of the Ultimate with humankind. It allows us to see the importance of the meeting of peoples and the contemporary interreligious encounter and dialogue. Although **that** dimension of our dialogical humanity has yet to penetrate the contours of global perception or the front pages of the daily newspapers, it has begun to silently transform the hearts and minds of human beings around the globe. Interreligious dialogue reveals that an aspect of the life of dialogue is the dialogue between religions. And at the heart of that meeting is the question of the meaning of the multiform traditions in relation to Transcendence/God/the Absolute. The conviction that human life is constituted by Transcendence is a common place of the great traditions and grounds our contention of unanimity among traditions concerning the common destiny of humanity in Transcendence. But it also raises the question of the meaning of those multiform traditions in relation to each other and the Ultimate.

As I have already indicated, the jury is still very much out on the question of whether or not this encounter of peoples will issue in a new world for humanity. Far too often, the results seem disastrous as these meetings of peoples, fueled by political and economic rivalries and the modern presumption to mastery over nature and humanity, lead to animosity and hostility. But this is neither the whole story nor its most telling aspect. What is most needed is some **orientation** in the midst of our shared situation towards what Radhakrishnan called this 'characteristic phenomenon' of our time. That orientation can arise from a deepened awareness of the dialogical structures of humanity itself as constituted by Transcendence.

The way to a deepened awareness of the dialogical structure of humanity has already been opened by two remarkable figures who earlier in the century pioneered the way in understanding dialogue. Here we wish to outline the philosophical anthropology that emerged in the work of these two pioneers. This will provide us with a grounding for our approach to the religious life of humankind and a foundation to further explore our thesis that the story of humankind is the making of humanity. Their philosophical anthropology also sheds light on our question of the destiny of humankind.

II

The two pioneers in articulating a dialogical philosophical anthropology of humanity are Martin Buber (1878-1967) and Eugen Rosenstock-Huessy (1888-1973). Buber is well-known for his book *Ich und Du*, translated as *I and Thou*. First published in 1923, the work has influenced a generation of

Western philosophy and Jewish and Christian theology.[8] Rosenstock-Huessy, on the other hand, has remained little known despite a corpus running to more than seven hundred books and articles.[9] Both had received classical German educations; both were profoundly shaken by the First World War, the collapse of German culture and the profound challenges posed to Western civilisation; both were part of similar circles of thought and reflection in post-War Germany; both had a Jewish ancestry although Rosenstock-Huessy became a Christian in his teens, while Buber became one of the most influential and well-known Jewish voices of our century. The significant point of intersection in their lives was what was then called their 'speech-thinking' or what I am calling here their shared dialogical anthropology.

Although both Buber and Rosenstock-Huessy had drunk deeply in their own ways at the fountains of German idealism,

---

8. Martin Buber, *I and Thou*, 2nd edn. New York: Charles Scribner's Sons, 1958. The association of Buber and Rosenstock-Huessy began in the 1920s in relation to the 'Frankfurt Union' and the journal *Die Kreatur* and continued into the 1960s. See Maurice Friedman, *Martin Buber's Life and Work*, 3 Vols., New York: E.P. Dutton, 1981, 1983. In relation to the Frankfurt Union, see Vol.I, pp. 277ff., and for *Die Kreatur* see Vol. II, pp. 106ff.

9. See Lise vander Molen, *A Complete Bibliography of the Writings of Eugen Rosenstock-Huessy*, Lewiston, NY: The Edwin Mellen Press, 1989. For an introduction to this important but little-known thinker, see M. Darrol Bryant and Hans Huessy (eds.), *Eugen Rosenstock-Huessy: Studies in his Life and Thought*, Lewiston, NY: The Edwin Mellen Press, 1986. For an interpretation of Martin Buber, mostly, and Eugen Rosenstock-Huessy that attempts to place them in a tradition of dialogical philosophy, see Shmuel Hugo Bergman, *Dialogical Philosophy: From Kierkegaard to Buber*, Albany, NY: State University of New York Press, 1991. However, Bergman's reading of Rosenstock-Huessy on pages 161-70 is limited and questionable.

they shared the conviction that the philosophical traditions of German idealism were not adequate to grasp the human conditions disclosed by the War and the collapse of European culture. Both were more sensitive to humanity's embeddedness in time and the sequence of generations than were those German and European idealists who treated humanity as a disembodied ego. As Rosenstock-Huessy wrote in the "Epilogue: The Survival Value of Humor" in his monumental work *Out of Revolution, Autobiography of Western Man*:

> My generation has survived pre-War decadence, the killing in the War, post-War anarchy, and revolutions, i.e., civil war. Today, before anybody awakens to conscious life in this narrowed world, unemployment, or airbomb-strafing, or class-revolutions, or lack of vitality, or lack of integration may have cast the die of his fate, and stamped him forever. We daily emerge out of social death by a miracle. Hence, we no longer care for Cartesian metaphysics. . . . We are groping for a social wisdom that leads beyond the brutal 'nomical' facts of economics and the monstrosities of the social volcano.[10]

And similarly, in *Ich und Du*, Buber eschews a separate 'world of ideas' and, instead, insists that he speaks of "nothing else but the real man, of you and of me, of our life and of our world — not of an I, or a state of being in itself alone."[11]

---

10. Eugen Rosenstock-Huessy, *Out of Revolution: The Autobiography of Western Man*, Norwich, VT: Argo Books, 1938, rpt. 1969, p. 757. In this remarkable text, Rosenstock-Huessy interprets the story of 'Western Man' as a single interrelated event of dialogue with destiny.

11. Martin Buber, *I and Thou*, p. 13. My gloss on Buber and Rosenstock-Huessy highlights elements of their work and gives centrality to the divine-human dialogue. It does so because I am not just seeking to present their views but to develop in concert with them a vision of the human in the Divine.

Both were persuaded that an adequate understanding of humanity must resonate in the lived experience of humanity as well as arise from attention to the unfolding life of humanity. These twin considerations turned their attention away from humanity absorbed in self-reflection or the Cartesian formula that affirmed 'I think therefore I am' and towards humanity in its relation life of being-with the earth, humanity, and the Ultimate.

Though Buber and Rosenstock-Huessy had shared the depths of the inhumanity revealed by the war, for neither did that horrendous experience utter the last word. Rather, it disclosed the necessity to turn again to fundamental questions to wrest anew the wisdom that was to be found at life's depths. Thus in philosophical and theological circles, just as in the realms of the arts, politics, and sciences, there was a reopening of fundamental questions in post-War Germany and across Europe. When Heidegger asserts in *Being and Time* that "it is fitting that we should raise anew the question of the meaning of Being,"[12] he speaks not only for himself but for his moment in the cultural life of post-War Europe. Humanity had become a question to itself, and it was thus essential to arrive at a renewed understanding of the human. Only that philosophical or existential wisdom could begin to point in another direction beyond the impasse of the moment. Yet it was essential that such wisdom be rooted in a profound understanding of humanity and the human venture, embodying the very depths of human nature.

That new direction was, curiously as we shall see, consonant with the oldest and deepest insights of Buber and Rosenstock-Huessy's respective traditions of faith, insights that had been eclipsed in modernity's affirmation of humanity's autonomy and mastery over nature. Indeed, it was these neglected sources of insight that provided the inspiration that gave rise to their shared vision of humanity as (1) constituted by the Divine and (2) grounded in and coming to be through dialogue. For both

12. Martin Heidegger, *Being and Time*, p. 19.

Buber and Rosenstock-Huessy, dialogue was not one among many human activities, nor mere academic exchange. Rather, in their understanding, life was dialogue. Dialogue was the name for the deepest and most profound relationship of humanity to reality.

While it is not possible here to explore in detail their respective understandings of dialogical humanity or to convey all the nuances of the differences in their views, it is possible to highlight three of the essential insights that emerge from their work. Those insights cluster around the themes of (1) the transcendent or divine presence which funds dialogue, (2) the centrality of dialogue to human life, and (3) the relational character of humanity as unfolded in time and space. Let us look at each of these in turn.

The Transcendent Presence

Buber and Rosenstock-Huessy shared with modern existentialists the philosophical presupposition that the analysis of the human condition must resonate with the actual experience of humanity. Yet there is a fundamental disagreement between Buber and Rosenstock-Huessy and the so-called secular existentialists like Martin Heidegger and Jean Paul Sartre. That disagreement concerns the constitution of that reality within which humanity finds itself. Are we here dealing with the classical metaphysical question of God/humanity/world or is it a question of humanity/world? This question is much disputed in relation to Heidegger: some read him with a Transcendent, others without. With Sartre, the issue is clearer: there is no transcendent or divine dimension. For Buber and Rosenstock-Huessy, humanity's life is life in relation to the Transcendent **and** the world. These three terms are not to be understood as pointing to three distinct realms or watertight compartments, nor should they be separated from the life experience they seek to evoke. For Buber and Rosenstock-Huessy, humanity finds itself in the given texture of the life of families, of societies, of traditions, of nature, **and** the Transcendent. And that Ultimate is simultaneously both other and present to our textured life in time.

One does not find traditional ontological or cosmological arguments on behalf of Transcendence in either Buber or Rosenstock-Huessy; indeed, both eschew such arguments as fruitless. Buber, for example, asserts that "the Eternal **Thou** can by its nature not become **It**. . . ."[13] Buber sees the process of reflection as inevitably transforming 'realities' into objects and thus distorting the reality of the human situation and that with which we have to do. Rather, Buber and Rosenstock-Huessy turn to the analysis of the human experience of life itself, especially in society and speech, to disclose its relation to Transcendence as the constituent ground of the phenomenon of humanity itself. As Buber was to remark in utter simplicity, 'living means being addressed.'[14] But the question of the source of this 'address' is what divides Buber and Rosenstock-Huessy from others within the existentialist movement with whom they shared a great deal.[15]

For Buber, it is this Transcendent Presence which is the basis for his description of human life as 'I-Thou' and 'I-It' relationships. Our humanity comes to be in response to the address of the Ultimate to be and become. For Rosenstock-Huessy "God is the I that always precedes our existence and the

---

13. Martin Buber, *I and Thou*, p. 112. His point is that we cannot make God an 'object' of thought, but that does not mean that God as constituting humanity cannot be acknowledged nor enter into our grammar of the human condition.

14. Martin Buber, *Between Man and Man*, London & Glasgow: Fontana Library, 1961, chapter on 'Dialogue,' p. 27.

15. For two important existentialist accounts, see M. Heidegger, *Being and Time*, *op. cit.*, and Jean Paul Sartre, *Being and Nothingness*, tr. by Hazel Barnes, New York: Philosophical Library, 1956.

existence of our fellow creatures."[16] And in his 'grammar' of human existence, humanity is 'the second person.'[17] Buber remarks that "meeting with God does not come to [man] in order that he may concern himself with God, but in order that he may confirm that there is meaning in the world."[18] While Rosenstock-Huessy shares this basic view, he is critical of the formulation 'I-Thou.' For Rosenstock-Huessy, this formulation obscures the precedence of the Divine Thou in the emergence of the I and the dynamic quality of the divine/human relation. It would be better to speak of Thou-I since it is the Divine that constitutes the Self, not the other way around. Rosenstock-Huessy was later to remark that Buber had spoken 'too early,' before the insights that were emerging in post-War Germany had fully ripened.[19] At the very least, Rosenstock-Huessy thought that the order of the formulation should be reversed — Thou-I rather than I-Thou — to underscore the awareness that the self comes to be in response to the reality Beyond — mediated through mothers and fathers, communities and traditions — which addresses us from the moment of our beginnings in time. In Rosenstock-Huessy's words:

> In our natural situation, that of being an addressee, we are neither active like the over-energetic Ego nor passive like the suffering under-dog. We are swimmers in a

---

16. Eugen Rosenstock-Huessy, *I am an Impure Thinker*, Norwich, VT: Argo Books, 1970, p. 11.
17. Eugen Rosenstock-Huessy, *I am an Impure Thinker*, p. 11. The same idea is developed in a different way in his *The Origin of Speech*, Norwich, VT: Argo Books, 1981, especially under the headings of the imperative and the social process of speech, see pp. 38 ff.
18. Martin Buber, *I and Thou*, p. 115.
19. See, for example, the editor's note in Eugen Rosenstock-Huessy, *Judaism Despite Christianity*, New York: Schocken Books, 1971, pp. 69-70.

> buoyant and everlasting medium. The dawn of creation is upon us, and we await our question, our specific mandate, in the silence of the beginnings of time. When we have learned to listen to the question and serve towards its solution, we have advanced to a new day.[20]

Thus if we fail to grasp the structure of humanity rightly, we cannot rightly understand the human situation. In the 'grammar' that emerges in Buber and Rosenstock-Huessy, that means that Transcendence is the **first person of a grammar of the human**.

The metaphor of 'grammar' is important here since both Buber and Rosenstock-Huessy eschewed idealist metaphysics for elevating thought over the actual. In Buber and Rosenstock-Huessy's hands, the quest for wisdom — philosophia — involved turning to life itself to uncover the dynamics and structures present to the human engagement with reality. Rosenstock-Huessy especially likened the task to that of the student of speech and language who seeks to become aware of the dynamics and structure of language — its grammar. But it is essential to remember that speaking and listening — the reality of language — precedes the grasp of its grammar just as here life itself precedes, and continually funds, the awareness and articulation of life's dynamics and structure: what we call here its grammar. Within this philosophical frame, dialogue as the relationship with reality always takes precedence over the articulation of that relationship in a 'grammar.' And the first person of that grammar that we find in Buber and Rosenstock-Huessy is the Transcendent, the Absolute, God.

Consequently, ours is not merely being-unto-death, as Heidegger suggested, but it is being-in-response to the address that comes through life itself. Nor is that 'address' — what Heidegger called 'Ruf' — which addresses humanity simply

---

20. Eugen Rosenstock-Huessy, *I am an Impure Thinker*, p. 12.

humanity itself, as Heidegger argued.[21] For Buber and Rosenstock-Huessy, we are addressed by the Beyond. In Buber's words, "In the signs of life which happens to us we are addressed. Who speaks?" And Buber's answer is this: "If we name the speaker of this speech God, then it is always the God of the moment, a moment God."[22] Buber's formulation is important in that it emphasises that God is not an object of thought, but a presence that 'speaks'. Moreover, God is 'a moment God' meaning that the Divine discloses itself in the moment of address, of meeting, of dialogue; God is not static in relation to humanity. This understanding does not mean, however, that Buber is anticipating process theology and its notion of a changing God. Rather, Buber's point is the dynamic of God for humanity: humanity finds itself in being addressed by Transcendence, and in response to that address, comes to be in an unfolding historical destiny. That destiny unfolds across generations, and it arises from the nexus of address and response.

What is significant for the purposes of this lecture is the way in which Buber and Rosenstock-Huessy portray the human situation. Humanity does not come to be in an empty universe but in one constituted by Transcendence. This relational ontology is constitutive of humanity as such. Thus at the heart of humanity lies the call to be and become not merely in relation to what is at hand or in terms of the present moment of technical society and its claims on our being and becoming, but in relation to the deeper ground of authentic life **in the present** in response to the Beyond. The present and the Beyond are not severed nor separated in Buber and Rosenstock-Huessy. They are interrelated moments in the dynamic unfolding of life; they constitute the fundamental terms in the grammar of life itself.

Although we have here focused on the divine-human

---

21. See Heidegger, *Being and Time*, especially pp. 269-80 where he affirms that the Ruf is the call of conscience.

22. Martin Buber, *I and Thou*, p. 32.

relationship, the 'world' is implicitly present in its two-fold meaning. 'World' is the name we give to both the realm of nature and to social reality.[23] For both Buber and Rosenstock-Huessy, the disorientation and turmoil that had overwhelmed Europe required an analysis that addressed the foundations of that disease rather than the symptoms. It is this fundamental analysis that is lacking in contemporary Western philosophy and is being eroded by the impact of the Western sciences and technologies of mastery that presume that the world exists from itself alone, an erosion that ends in nihilism. Once, however, the divine-human structure of human being is brought to the fore, then the world can come into proper view.

Dialogical Humanity

If, as Buber and Rosenstock-Huessy argued, the human situation is rightly portrayed as one constituted by humanity-in-relation to Transcendence, then we can understand why dialogue becomes the name for the life of humanity. For in this account of things, humanity unfolds in a dialogical relationship with the divine, the world, and the human. But of course this way of putting the matter is misleading: the clarity and sequence of the terms belies the all-at-onceness of the experience of life. Few knew this problem better than Rosenstock-Huessy who attempted in his grammar of human life to respect simultaneously the particular in the universal and *vice-versa*. Both Rosenstock-Huessy and Buber recognised that humanity does not move in a neat or

23. The issue here is what Raimon Panikkar was later to call a 'cosmotheandric vision of reality.' Although we have here focused on the 'theandric' dimensions with only some few references to the 'cosmo' aspects, that aspect has not been far from my mind. For a fuller study of Panikkar see the PhD dissertation of L. Anthony Savari Raj, *The Cosmotheandric Vision of Raimon Panikkar: A Study*, Radhakrishnan Institute for Advanced Studies in Philosophy, University of Madras, 1994.

ordered way from the divine to the world and to one another. Rather, we, as particular human beings and communities, find ourselves emerging in the complex emotional dynamics of family life attempting to discern there the words that make for life and growth. We are in the midst of larger social institutions and processes and are there deluged with claims and counter-claims of what makes for significant living. We find ourselves as members of political societies with their claims for the appropriate ways to use and deploy power. We find ourselves caught up in the vicissitudes of our historical moment and its insights and pretenses. Which claims are to be acknowledged, which rejected, which ignored? But switching our focus from the general to the particular does not alter the essential philosophical point, though it does complicate and texture it. That point is the dialogical character of the human situation.

Few have been able to unfold the dialogical character of the human situation as ably as Rosenstock-Huessy. Unfortunately, we can only hint at that achievement here. To begin, it is important to note that his is a more complex grammar of dialogical humanity than Buber's. Buber's two-foldedness — I-Thou, I-It — becomes four-foldedness in Rosenstock-Huessy — humanity in dialogue with the Future, Past, Inner, and Outer fronts of life. For Rosenstock-Huessy, that dialogue of humanity with life and its transcendent foundation unfolds in a four-fold or cruciform structure, pattern, and dynamic.[24] Humanity is, in his view, faced inward and outward, forward and backward simultaneously. Each of these fronts of life — in space from within to without, in time from backward to forward — confronts

24. For a fuller exposition of Eugen Rosenstock-Huessy's views on this point, see my "Toward a Grammar of the Spirit in Society," in *The Many Faces of Religion and Society*, ed. by M.D. Bryant and Rita Mataragnon, New York: Paragon House, 1985, pp. 173-90 and "The Grammar of the Spirit: Time, Speech, and Society," in *Eugen Rosenstock-Huessy: Studies in His Life and Thought*, ed. by M. D. Bryant & Hans Huessy, *op. cit.*, pp. 233-60.

the human with the demands of dialogue. In time, we are confronted with the question of what from the past we must hold on to and what we must let go of; in our response to these challenges, we write the story of our generation and era. Similarly, in space we turn **in** to the demands of the self and **out** to the realm of nature and society. And here too we must respond to the claims that come to us from within and without. Thus Rosenstock-Huessy's formula for humanity's dialogue with itself, others and nature, the past and the future, the heavens and the earth, is 'respondeo etsi mutabor': I respond although I will be changed.[25]

The dialogical character of human being and becoming is, as we have already shown, unfolded in the order of space and time. Indeed, it is basic to life itself. Thus Buber remarked that,

> The life of dialogue is no privilege of intellectual activity like dialectic. It does not begin in the upper story of humanity. It begins no higher than where humanity begins. There are not gifted and ungifted here, only those who give themselves and those who withhold themselves.[26]

While Buber tended to focus more on the dialogue between 'I' and 'Thou,' Rosenstock-Huessy gave more attention to the dialogical character of human life as it unfolds in space and time. That unfolding is neither automatic nor mechanical but passes through the human person who responds in countless varieties of ways. The point here is not those varieties but rather the relationships that are given in the life of humanity.

For dialogical humanity, meaning grows out of the life of dialogue with Transcendence, the world, and other human beings. Meaning is constituted by relationships rather than concepts. When humanity finds itself in vital relationships with

---

25. Eugen Rosenstock-Huessy, *I am an Impure Thinker*, pp. 10ff.
26. Buber, *Between Man & Man*, p. 54.

the Transcendent, mediated through communities of faith, or through the world given to us in creation and society, or through the other as humanity in its gender and cultural diversity, then life becomes awash with meaning. But when humanity is experienced as isolated in a silent cosmos, or as alienated from the worlds of society and creation, or as alone in relation to the other, then meaning evaporates and our humanity shrinks. It is relation that bestows meaning.

Thus our dialogical humanity is constituted by dialogue and relation. Indeed, these are so deeply intertwined that it is only for purposes of analysis that they can be distinguished. Hence the discussion of the centrality of dialogue to the human venture leads inextricably into an outline of relational humanity.

Relational Humanity

The centrality of relationship to the philosophical anthropology of both Buber and Rosenstock-Huessy is immediately obvious in the classic statement with which Buber opens *Ich und Du*:

> To man the world is twofold, in accordance with his twofold attitude. The attitude of man is twofold, in accordance with the twofold nature of the primary words which he speaks. The primary words are not isolated words, but combined words. The one primary word is the combination *I-Thou*.
>
> The other primary word is the combination I-it . . .[27]

---

27. Martin Buber, *I and Thou*, p. 3. See also Martin Buber, *A Believing Humanism: My Testament 1902-1965*, tr. by Maurice Friedman, New York: Simon and Schuster, 1967, p. 201 where he writes, "The crisis of man which has become apparent in our day announces itself most clearly as a crisis of trust. . . . And the crisis of speech is bound up with this loss of trust. . . . Therefore, the fact that it is so difficult for present-day man to pray. . . and the fact that it is so difficult for him to carry on a →

Thus the formulations 'I-Thou' and 'I-It' entered the language of philosophical anthropology. In his early writing, Buber's I-Thou/ I-It come to signify two basic attitudes towards life as well as the twofold relationship to life present in/to every human being. This relational understanding of the human was fundamental to both Buber and Rosenstock-Huessy's work, even though the latter would speak of those relationships, as we have already indicated, in a more differentiated way.

Buber and Rosenstock-Huessy saw the profound limitations of a philosophical tradition founded on the Cartesian dictum that because we think we are. They did, however, share with Hegel an awareness of the horizon of temporality and with Nietzsche a concern for the living moment. But Buber and Rosenstock-Huessy brought to their analysis of these themes a distinctive awareness that was rooted in their sensitivity to speech as the vital key to living humanity. It was precisely speech in its particularity — rather than reflection in its generality—that embodied humanity's response to the historical moment in which life in all its wretchedness and glory was being unfolded.

For Buber, it was a two-fold humanity; for Rosenstock-Huessy it was a four-fold humanity. For Buber, the human either faced the mystery of the Thou or lived in the world of It. Despite Buber's efforts to acknowledge something valid in the 'I/It' relation, it always comes through as second best and lacking in its basic character. For Rosenstock-Huessy, our relationships extend without and within in space, forward and

---

→ genuine talk with his fellow men are elements of a single set of facts. This lack of trust in Being . . . points to an innermost sickness of the sense of existence." Here Buber points to the interior connection between the relation to the Transcendent and one another. It is a point worth pondering and crucial to the argument here for the relationship of the Transcendent to humanity.

backward in time as well as above and below into the eternal. This remarkably enriched account of the relational character of the human points to the many fronts of dialogue that arise at the many fronts of life. When the multiplicity, or in Rosenstock-Huessy's preferred word, the multiformity of humanity is unfolded, then our awareness deepens. Humanity is not just this one thing, but a constellation of relationships that spans the relation we have to ourselves, to the relationship we have to the earth, and the relationship we have with those who came before us and those who will come after us. It is when humanity is thus restored to the multiform relations of life that meaning can emerge. Alienated from those life forms and patterns of exchange between humanity and life, humanity becomes a stranger to itself. Lost in the world of abstractions rather than enmeshed in a life of thought, alienated in a world of commodities rather than alive in a world of exchange, caught in the merry-go-rounds of emotional trauma rather than flowing with the movement of life, humanity becomes estranged from its moorings.

But when humanity finds itself in the world of relations, then community is given to humanity. For both Buber and Rosenstock-Huessy, community is not another category alongside the human but rather the inevitable form of our relational humanity.[28]

In both Buber and Rosenstock-Huessy, then, it was humanity-in-dialogue that constituted the ground of life and the fundamental category for a philosophical anthropology. When they brought forward the centrality of dialogue to the understanding of the human, they were charting waters that had not been charted before even though they had been sounded

28. See Eugen Rosenstock-Huessy, *Speech and Reality*, Norwich, VT: Argo Books, 1970, especially "In Defense of the Grammatical Method," pp. 9-44, and Martin Buber, *Between Man and Man*, especially his distinctions between community and collective, pp. 144ff.

in the religious heritage of humankind. Although the work of Buber and Rosenstock-Huessy does not provide us with either a finished agenda or a completed map of humanity, it does provide us with a fresh articulation of an ancient wisdom: namely, that humanity is constituted by the Ultimate. Moreover, their insights into dialogical humanity allow us to begin to discern meanings and hear notes that might alter our understanding of what is unfolding in the midst of the events that shape our age. The heart of their contribution is the orientation they provide. We may not yet see clearly or face to face, but perhaps we can heed those notes that call us to take our place in the yet unfinished melody of humanity in relation to itself and that Beyond that funds it all.

III

Seen in the light of the dialogical account of humanity pioneered by Buber and Rosenstock-Huessy, the religious and spiritual traditions of humankind emerge as the living response of humanity's life of dialogue with the Transcendent, the Unmanifest. In that dialogue, the initiative rests as much Beyond as Within. The Transcendent has been revealed or disclosed and named in diverse names — names that are so holy that we should tremble to even utter them — in the manifold traditions of religious life: Yahweh, Brāhmaṇa, God, Tao, Allāh, Emptiness, Kitche Manitou, Ek Oṁkār. . . . Thus the religious traditions reveal a shared awareness that humanity unfolds in dialogue with the Absolute which simultaneously exceeds the quotidian while being none the less present to life in time. Those dialogues with the Ultimate have been enfolded in the religious traditions of humankind. And the contemporary encounter and dialogue between religions can be seen as encountering and exploring across tradition the deepest wisdom given to humanity. But such dialogue must be, as Buber remarked, authentic:

> There is genuine dialogue—no matter whether spoken

> or silent — where each of the participants really has in mind the other or others in their present and particular being and turns to them with the intention of establishing a living mutual relation between himself and them. There is technical dialogue, which is prompted solely by the need of objective understanding. And there is monologue disguised as dialogue, in which two or more men, meeting in space, speak each with himself in strangely tortuous and circuitous ways and yet imagine they have escaped the torment of being thrown back on their own resources.[29]

Genuine dialogue is an intrahuman as well as an interreligious dialogue concerning dialogue with the Ultimate. The diverse traditions have unfolded their respective grammars of their respective dialogical encounters with the Beyond. But prior to the present age, those understandings, practices, and grammars have lived in relative isolation from one another. And meeting often led to hostility. However, that isolation is increasingly broken by the social conditions of the modern and post-modern age. The irony is that within the context of a dialogical understanding of the human condition, the religious traditions need not remain isolated but can enter a fruitful relationship with one another at the deepest levels. Such an encounter and dialogue need not — indeed, must not — issue in syncretism or relativism but in a revitalised awareness of humanity in relation to the Divine. A post-modern necessity is an awareness of the multiform ways to live profoundly in relation to that reality which funds us, transcends us and calls us to be. The revelations of the Whole given fully in a particular Way must respect the Ways given to others.

---

29. Martin Buber, *Between Man and Man*, p. 37, though the language here is not what we now call 'inclusive,' Buber's intent was not exclusive or limited to the male gender.

Already in 1929, Buber had written that

> A time of genuine religious conversations is beginning — not those so-called but fictitious conversations where none regarded and addressed his partner in reality, but genuine dialogues, speech from certainty to certainty, but also from one open-hearted person to another open-hearted person. Only then will genuine common life appear, not that of an identical content of faith which is alleged to be found in all religions, but that of the situation of anguish and of expectation.[30]

Given the vision of dialogical humanity that we have outlined here, such a conviction is not surprising. Tragically, the emergence of Nazi Germany not only delayed those 'genuine religious conversations' — which had already begun to emerge in the relations between Jews like Martin Buber and Franz Rosenzweig and Christians like Rosenstock-Huessy and Joseph Wittig — but showed the terrible price of the failure to recognise and acknowledge our dialogical humanity. As the lust for mastery over others disclosed its diabolical face, the necessity of a different understanding of humanity emerged as an imperative. The same point has been made by Richard Rubenstein in the conclusion to his important but disturbing study that chronicles the depths of inhumanity that lurk behind public policies in our century, *The Age of Triage: Fear and Hope in an Overcrowded World*.

> In this new political and social environment, our worst pollution may very well be what we do to ourselves. That is why a religious transformation is crucial. But, if it is to come, it must be an inclusive vision appropriate to a global civilisation in which Moses and Muhammad, Christ, Buddha, and Confucius all play a role. We can no longer rest content with a humanity divided into the

---

30. Martin Buber, *Between Man and Man*, p. 24.

> working and the workless, the saved and the damned, the Occident and the Orient. Our fates are too deeply intertwined.[31]

But for such an inclusive vision to emerge, humanity must rediscover itself in dialogue with life's depths as well as with those with whom one shares the planet. The call for religious transformation rests implicitly on a recognition of dialogical humanity.

It is appropriate that such dialogue begins between the religions as the keepers of the most profound wisdom of the dialogue between the Divine Unmanifest and humanity. The religious traditions have recognised, each in their own distinctive ways, that the experience of humanity is always revelational, that is, a disclosing. And as humanity heeds and responds, a tradition of life is called into being, a spiritual type is created. The point here is that the specific grammars, practices, and Way of a given tradition create both a specific type as well as a shared awareness that the matrix of human being and becoming is in dialogue, in the crucible of Transcendence. Such knowing is existential and spiritual rather than informational. Such knowing touches the depths of humanity and calls it into being. Already in *Ich und Du*, Buber points out that "all revelation is summons and sending."[32] And in Rosenstock-Huessy, it is the hearing of the Imperative that calls us into being. Hearing and heeding the Imperative, writes Rosenstock-Huessy, "the things of the world are mastered, times are decided, people are made by it."[33]

---

31. Richard Rubenstein, *The Age of Triage*, p. 240.

32. Martin Buber, *I and Thou*, p. 115.

33. Eugen Rosenstock-Huessy, *The Origin of Speech*, p. 54. Here, Rosenstock-Huessy outlines what he calls the 'full cycle of speech' as it moves from the imperative (or dramatic) to the subjunctive (or lyrical) to the epical (or narrative) and ends in the logical (or classifying). As he remarks here: "the imperative, →

The classical traditions of wisdom in the East and West have placed the divine-human relationship at the heart of reality and their respective quests for wisdom. The quest for the human is inextricably linked to the quest for the divine and the quest for the divine goes through the interior of the human. This is the wisdom that is given in that relationship known as 'revelation' — whether given in the texts of sacred scriptures or the enlightenment of the human heart. Thus the great nurseries of humankind have been the religious traditions that have addressed and shaped humanity throughout time — and continue to do so today despite the troubling inroads of secularity. The little and great traditions form the human along the lines of what is **given** to them in their encounter and dialogue with the Ultimate. For the Jew, it is the revelation of the Torah and a covenanted community that lies at the heart of spiritual wisdom; for the Buddhist, it is the aspiration towards Enlightenment on the basis of meditational practice that is core to what has been given — not as a mere set of ideas or practices but as a way to Transcendence. For the Hindu, it is the awareness that we finally move beyond dualisms to a unity with the Ultimate that transcends all divisions. And so on and so forth.

These traditions constitute the grammars of the spirit that have long turned humanity towards its deepest encounters with the real and with itself. These traditions are profound encounters with the Absolute where the disclosure reshapes humanity in the likeness and image of the Absolute given in a particular tradition. In earlier eras, the formation of the human in the image and likeness of the Absolute unfolded in isolation; now we have become aware of one another. And that continuing process of the making of humanity needs to be done in concert so that our

---

→ the most ancient sentence, trans-substantiates the world." This understanding of the full cycle of speech is another argument for the primacy of the Transcendent in the grammar of human life.

emergent planetary humanity can heed again the call from Beyond that gives us our deepest wisdom and most abiding direction. That process within the body of humanity will be deepened as we become more attuned to the crucible of Transcendence that is at the true centre of the life of humanity. It is in that crucible that we learn anew that it is in the encounter and dialogue with Transcendence that we realise our destiny. Such an understanding of **humanum** has already been anticipated and marked out in the writings of pioneers like Martin Buber and Eugen Rosenstock-Huessy; and it is there implicitly in the great traditions of religious and spiritual life.[34]

---

34. In the next lecture, I attempt to point to some of those anticipations assuming the general point made here. In other words, my expositions of the religious traditions simply assumes this crucible of the Unmanifest Transcendent that I have attempted to unfold here.

3

The Making of Humanity in the Multiform Religious Traditions

All things return to God . . .
However, human beings do not enter the world as full-fledged divine forms.[1]

IN the earlier lectures, we offered an anticipatory sketch of divine-human destiny and outlined a contemporary understanding of dialogical humanity in the crucible of Transcendence. At the conclusion of that lecture, we suggested that we could see the multiform religious traditions as 'dialogues with Transcendence' that formed pathways for the making of humanity.[2] Here, then, we

1. William Chittick, *The Sufi Path of Knowledge*, Albany, NY: SUNY Press, 1992, pp. 19-20.
2. This is not intended to reduce theology to anthropology or as anthropocentrism except in the sense that the making of humanity in the context of creation is central (not exclusive) to the historical drama. Rather, I am attempting to argue that the quest for God is simultaneously the making of humanity as that is unfolded in the crucible and dynamics of life itself. The charge of reducing theology to anthropology rests on making a distinction and separation that I find unhelpful. The point is made in a different way in the writings of Raimundo Panikkar where he speaks about the 'cosmotheandric' vision of reality, one which attempts to break with the sharp separations of cosmic-divine-human in favour of an integral vision of reality. See the Ph.D. thesis of L. Anthony Savari Raj, "The Cosmotheandric Vision of Raimon Panikkar," Madras University, 1994.

want to look at those multiform religious traditions in more detail.

I

This lecture will attempt to give more content to our thesis that the religious life of humankind is integral to the story of the making of humanity. As we turn our attention to the multiple religious forms, we do well to recall two axioms that are crucial to our argument. First, we assume that humanity is one but multiform. And secondly, we believe that the religious traditions seek to return us or lead us to the Ultimate. When these two axioms are linked to one another, we can see that the religious traditions in their historical manifestations are the principle matrices ('matrix,' 'mother,' 'womb') for the making of humanity in relation to the Ultimate within the order of time. We will not be able to sketch all the multiform ways and spiritual types that are to be found within the religious history of humankind. Instead, we will confine our attention to six great traditions: Hindu, Buddhist, Christian, Muslim, Confucian and Sikh.[3] Moreover, even within this restriction, we will not be able to attend to the variety found within each tradition, but rather

3. By discussing these six traditions, I am not excluding others. I believe that my thesis is relevant there too. It might, however, be argued, on the evidence of history, that religions have historically limited roles. We know, for example, that throughout history we have seen the emergence and disappearance of religious traditions. Consider, for example, the Greek religions of the pre-Christian era or the Nordic religions. Both of these traditions are known to us only in their mythologies and not, any more, as living traditions. Some other traditions, like the Native traditions of North America, suffered profoundly from their encounter with Europeans who decimated the indigenous populations and demeaned their religions. But, in this instance, there has been a recent resurgence of these First-peoples traditions.

content ourselves with a brief sketch of the tradition and its human-divine heart, the distinctive spiritual type it calls into being through its own distinct complex of practices, rituals, beliefs, and values. Each tradition is **a way to the Ultimate**, but it is **simultaneously a way of making humanity**.

The inner spiritual heart of each Way cannot be approached directly, but only indirectly through the scriptures, words, symbols, rituals, practices, and stories of a given tradition. Thus in our exposition, it will be these phenomenal aspects of a given Way that will be our access to its inner spiritual heart.[4] It must also be acknowledged that the historical unfolding of a given Way to the Ultimate is profoundly ambiguous within historical time. The religious life of the Way itself is often caught within that very ignorance, sin, disharmony, suffering and grasping that a given Way seeks to remedy.[5] Thus in the historical record,

---

4. The point here is not the familiar 'insider/outsider' distinction so fundamental to the modern study of religion. It is rather a more general point concerning accounts of faiths either by insiders or outsiders. We have to go to the inner heart of every tradition through its language, rituals, practices and beliefs. Thus as a Christian I may not claim a privileged 'insider' status for my account of the Christian Way, since my presentation of my own tradition is also subject to the same limitations as my accounts of other traditions: namely, that in speaking about a tradition, one must appeal primarily to that which is publicly available, hoping one's treatment of those outer dimensions of a tradition can point us to its interior and spiritual dimensions. As a believer in a given tradition, one may be grasped by the tradition, but a reflective account of that tradition appeals to the public dimensions of that tradition.

5. This is the irony of religion: that it participates in the very human problematic it is intended to overcome or to transform. This results in the often profound ambiguity of religious traditions in their historical life and unfolding. See, for example, Paul Tillich, *Systematic Theology*. Vol. I., Chicago: University of Chicago Press, 1951, especially the sections where he →

we encounter the profound ambiguity of religion as witness to the Ultimate and bearer of the divine yet caught in sin, ignorance, the lust for power, pettiness, greed, etc. Indeed, there are times in the history of religion that these ambiguities have virtually overwhelmed the particular Way. These moments and periods have been so profound that they have left only a dim echo of the life-giving Way or its inspired purposes. Thus the history of the religious life of humankind is marked by periodic renewals that recover the earlier pathway. Such periods of renewal are to be found in every tradition.

As I have already indicated, we are here approaching the religious pathways of humankind as the matrix for the making of humanity. That making is a spiritual process that unfolds in, with, and under the practices, rituals, beliefs, and values of a given religious tradition. It is in the religious traditions that, to use Edwards' language, one encounters knowledge, being and joy of the One who seeks communion with creation. The process of making humanity shares, across tradition, a common end. That end is human transcendence or the realisation or fulfilment of humanity in the divine. It is the Ultimate that is 'the further shore.'[6] This ultimate end, as we have already indicated, is not

→ discusses the human situation under the headings of "The Basic Ontological Structure," "The Ontological Elements," and "Being and Finitude," pp. 163-203, and Gregory Baum, *Religion and Alienation*, New York: Paulist Press, 1975, especially the chapters on "The Ambiguity of Religion: A Biblical Account" and "The Ambiguity of Religion: A Social Science Account," pp. 62-114.

6. The phrase is found in a number of different sources. My reference is to the title of a volume by the remarkable Father Henri LeSaux/Swami Abishiktananda, *The Further Shore*, Delhi: ISPCK, 1975, rpt. 1984. See also my review of his *The Secret of Arunachala: A Christian Hermit on Shiva*'s *Holy Mountain* in *Dialogue and Alliance*, Vol. 3, No. 4, 1989-90, pp. 81-3.

to be separated from the bodily-existential-cosmic dimensions of human life and its unfolding. It is the life of the human spirit unfolding towards its proper end: Liberation (*mokṣa*), Enlightenment (*nirvāṇa*), Salvation (Salvus), Submission (Islam), Propriety (Li) and Ecstatic Singing of the Divine Name (Nāmjap). Each of these ends entails, in the understandings of the distinctive traditions themselves, the full realisation of the human and of that which lies Beyond. Is not the attainment of Enlightenment the proper end of that *anatta*/not-self that we are? And is this equivalent to the Christian end of salvation/ *salvus*?

Unlike some interpreters of the religious life of humankind, I am not persuaded that these varied understandings of the end or goal of human striving can be collapsed into one or that they are all different names for the same thing. Rather, we better see them in their own terms, namely, as distinctive pathways to the Ultimate that contribute in their own way to the making of polyphonic humankind.[7] If unity were singularity, there would

---

7. It is necessary to insist upon this point, especially in India where there is a too easy tendency to claim, mainly in Vedāntic circles, that 'all religions are the same.' This is not my claim. Moreover, the very meaning of this phrase needs to be clarified. It has its origin in the Vedas and refers to the variety of worship forms within the Vedic traditions that bring one to the Beyond; its reference is **not** to the variety of world religious traditions. And even in the context of the religions, to say that religions have a common end, namely, to lead one to the Absolute, is not to say either that they are the same or even that it is the same face of the Absolute that one encounters in all the religions. Nor is it adequate to affirm that the true heart of all religions is the Advaitic experience of non-duality, as Vivekānanda does. (See Anantanand Rambachan, "Svāmī Vivekānanda: A Hindu Model for Interreligious Dialogue," pp. 9-19, M.D. Bryant & F.K. Flinn, *Interreligious Dialogue: Voices from a New Frontier*, *op.cit.*, where he makes this point concerning Vivekānanda.) Rather, my point is the historical →

be no unity to be sought. Unity contains within itself multiformity or internal diversity. This is most obvious in relation to humanity where there is not only the multiformity of female and male but also intergenerational multiformity and multiform spiritual types. Yet humanity is one. We need to realise that we are not only enriched by this diversity, but that it is through this very multiformity that the unity of humankind is achieved.

When I below speak of the distinctive spiritual types found in each tradition or Way, it is not meant to deny analogues and similarities across tradition.[8] Rather the distinctiveness lies in the gift of the Ultimate given in **the configuration of elements**,

---

→ fact that the religions themselves identify their end as something Beyond. But I also acknowledge that their respective accounts of the Beyond vary profoundly. And it is, I believe, essential that we hear those differences and not collapse them into merely different words for or worship of the same thing. The different faces of the Absolute that are disclosed to us in the religious traditions have diverse impacts on us as human beings. Although it should not be necessary, it must be said that our list of traditions is neither exhaustive nor meant to be exhaustive.

8. It is important not to mystify the term 'type.' It is always under our noses. When I speak of 'type,' I do not speak about it as an 'ideal' but as what is right before our eyes. It is becoming who we are as sons and daughters, brothers and sisters, husbands and wives, mothers and fathers, as persons who become in the Way given us in our respective religious traditions. These are the great human types that we are continually making and remaking in the unfolding of generations. And those types are formed within the respective wombs of the religious traditions which form 'mothers' and 'Confucian mothers,' 'fathers' and 'Sikh fathers,' sons and 'Jewish sons,' 'daughters' and 'Hindu daughters.' Religious traditions seek the holiness/wholeness of humanity as that is given in the depth of each tradition as it forms and remakes our humanity in the crucible of its particular Way to the Ultimate.

not in the elements themselves.[9] That there are, for example, mystics in every tradition is obvious, just as there are devotional *bhaktas* and more active doers. But is the Muslim mystic the same as the Hindu mystic, the Shin-Buddhist faith the same as the Lutheran-Christian faith, the Taoist meditator the same as the Jain meditator, the Sikh *bhakta* the same as the Jewish devotee? The question is complex. Part of the confusion lies in the failure to distinguish between types found within the religious traditions from the religious tradition itself. There are places of meeting across religions as the types within —*jñāna*, *bhakti*, *karma*, and *raj* to use the names given in the Hindu Way—meet one another and recognise their kinship across the differences of tradition. But those differences of tradition are not merely external and thus to be discarded in the twinkling of the eye. They are integral to what we have become and what we have been given of the Ultimate. Thus the differences remain, not as oppositions but as a sacred gift on the shared pilgrimage of humanity towards its end in the Ultimate. Moreover, where the meeting is profound there is a recognition that that shared across tradition can revive, renew each, and bring to the other the distinctive gifts of each. Thus, the practitioner of the moral/kārmic way recognises his or her brother/sister whether in Puritan garb or a Chinese robe. The mystic knows the mystic whether clothed in the yellow robes of the Sri Lankan monk or the lama-haired pancho of the Peruvian shaman or the grey suit of the Danish mystic. The intra-religious types are not confined to particular traditions, nor are they coterminus with the boundaries of cultures. They recognise each other across these boundaries. Nevertheless, these affinities do not eliminate the differences represented by the names of the great traditions: Hindu, Buddhist, Confucian, Jain, Jewish, Taoist, Christian, Muslim, Sikh and others.

---

9. This point is not as clear as I would like, but it is as clear as I can make it now.

As humans, we share one humanity with all other human beings, but our humanity can be — and is — configured in diverse ways, ways that constitute distinctive religious as well as intra-religious types. It is in those configurations that we come to be as Hindus, Muslims, Christians, Buddhists, Confucianists, and Sikhs.

There are of course other aspects of cultural/historical life that shape humanity, but here the focus is on the role of religions in that humanity-making project.[10] Central to that process is the notion of spiritual types or forms. The term 'type' must not be understood in a cookie-cutter sense. By type I mean the multiform spiritual types that are given to us in the names of the different Ways. It is essential to see that spiritual types — Ibn al-Arabi called them 'divine forms' — are neither genetic nor material, but spiritual and potential. They provide a spiritual form for humanity to realise itself in relation to the Divine. But they are actualised through human freedom. In this sense, they are analogous to what Protestant Christianity described as a 'vocation' or 'calling.' Just as a vocation requires a human response, the type remains hidden and unrealised without a human response; without human response they remain seeds unsprouted. These spiritual types constitute the deepest core of a tradition. They are partially realised by all in a given tradition and fully realised when we speak of persons who are, for example, 'Realised Souls' in Hinduism, or Bodhisattvas and Arhants in Buddhism, or Christ-like in Christianity.

10. For a fuller discussion of these matters, see the following chapter and especially the discussion of the grammar of the spirit found in the work of Eugen Rosenstock-Huessy. On the notion of 'type' as used here, let me add that the primary sense takes precedence over the secondary sense of type discussed above and found in the literature of the sociology of religion where the priest, prophet, charismatic, mystic, and activist are often spoken of as religious types. But this is an internal differentiation within traditions and not what I am seeking to point to when I use the larger notion of 'spiritual type.'

With these preliminary observations in mind, let us briefly unfold the Ways given to us in the great traditions of religious life.[11] We will begin with the Hindu Way as the oldest example of a Way to the Ultimate that has given us a distinctive spiritual type: the Hindu.

II

THE HINDU WAY: MANY PATHS, ONE GOAL

I wish to place over this brief presentation of the Hindu Way two texts:

From the *Īśa Upaniṣad*:

Behold the universe in the glory of God:
and all that lives and moves on earth.
    Leaving the transient,
    find joy in the Eternal:
set not your heart on another's possession.[12]

From the *Bhagavad Gītā*:

Many are the forms of the living,
Many the wombs that bear them.[13]

---

11. For the accounts that follow, I am grateful to a host of scholars who have made the world's traditions of faith available to us. I want especially to acknowledge my gratitude to Huston Smith, whose then *Religions of Man* (1957), now *The World's Religions* (new edn., 1991) was my first introduction to the living faiths. It is still, in my view, the best introduction. See also Ninian Smart, *The World's Religions*, Englewood Cliffs, NJ: Prentice Hall, 1989 and Mary Pat Fisher, *Living Religions*, 2nd edn., Englewood Cliffs, NJ: Prentice Hall, 1993.
12. *Īśa Upaniṣad* in *The Upaniṣads*, ed. by Juan Mascaro, Harmondsworth: Penquin, 1973, p. 19. All the citations from the Upaniṣads are from this edition unless otherwise indicated.
13. *Bhagavad Gītā*, XIV, 17-18.

Perhaps no tradition is as great a challenge to our vision as the internal diversity of the Hindu Way. It is a challenge in that it presents such an array of practices, rituals, beliefs, and values, that it is difficult to see the Hindu type at the heart of these manifold paths. At the same time, this tradition offers the clearest example of the multiplicity of existential ways to the type that is central to a given religious tradition. It reveals a unity in diversity. Yet Hindu divines have always insisted, rightly I believe, on the unity that permeates this diversity. The unity lies in the goal, which is symbolised as Liberation or *mokṣa*.[14] The principle obstacles to the goal of liberation are described in the Hindu traditions as ignorance and attachment. The ignorance is not pedestrian but profound: it is the ignorance that hides our true nature. And the wisdom that is an antidote to this ignorance is not primarily an idea but the truth to be realised in experience. To become a realised soul, a great soul, to realise the identity of the Self and the Absolute is the great end of life's journey in the Hindu way.

But the Hindu way immediately contextualises its own deepest wisdom by recognising that within humanity there are a plurality of dispositions: the intellectual, emotional, actional, and experimental. For each, there is an appropriate discipline or *yoga* through which one could achieve realisation or *mokṣa*. Those are *jñāna-yoga*, *bhakti-yoga*, *karma-yoga*, and *rāj-yoga*.[15] Thus these different *yoga*s can be cultivated by different people in accordance with their dominant disposition. Each discipline suits a particular dominant temperment, but all have a common goal: to aid the disciple in reaching and realising the Ultimate.

The beginnings of the Hindu way are beyond the reach of our

---

14. For a discussion of *mokṣa* see R. Balasubramanian, *Advaita Vedānta*, Madras: University of Madras, 1976, pp. 249 ff.

15. For a brief introduction to these four *yogas*, see Huston Smith, *The World's Religions*, *op.cit.*, pp. 26-50.

historical consciousness. Tradition believes that the Hindu way emerges in time prior to the third century BC. Its oldest Scriptures are the Vedas (*c.* 2000 BC). Then there are the Upaniṣads (800-400 BC), the Epics (400 BC-AD 200) and the Purāṇas (AD 1000-1500). Over the course of time, many streams of Hindu life emerged. Sometimes they were related to particular Hindu deities; at other times they were related to particular realised souls. The vast mythological, ritual, convictional, and practical resources of the Hindu Way achieved particular configurations that moved the hearts and minds of communities of Hindu believers. There is no institutional mentality within Hinduism, and so the spiritual relationship between *guru* and disciple always remains central to the Hindu Way.[16] The making of the Hindu is thus a living spiritual propagation from *guru* to disciple, generation after generation.

In this tradition, the human problem is ignorance and attachment. The ignorance is profound. It veils the truth of things, especially the truth of the Self or *ātman*. Thus humanity is caught in *māyā* or 'illusion.' But the *māyā* is appealing to our lost and ignorant humanity and so we become attached to it in a myriad of ways — from confusing the body with the Self to attachment to power, when it too is passing. The antidote to this ignorance and attachment is the realisation that the Self is all, is the God within. Thus the *Īśa Upaniṣad* reminds us that one "who sees all beings in his own Self, and his own Self in all beings, loses all fear. When a sage sees this great Unity and his Self has become all beings, what delusion and what sorrow can ever be near him?"[17] But while caught in ignorance and attachment, we

16. See, for example, the discussion of *guru* and disciple in Swami Abhishiktananda, *Guru and Disciple*, London: SPCK, 1974. For an interesting study of the attempt to adapt the *guru* tradition to Christianity see Catherine Cornille, *The Guru in Indian Catholicism*, Louvain: Peeters Press, 1991.

17. *Īśa Upaniṣad*, p. 49.

do not realise that "always dwelling within all beings is the *ātman*, the *puruṣa*, the Self, a little flame in the heart."[18] And it is, says the *Māṇḍūkya Upaniṣad*, this *ātman*, the Spirit itself, that is "the end of evolution and non-duality. He is peace and love."[19] Or as it says in the *Chāndogya Upaniṣad*, the one "who on this earth finds and knows *ātman*, his own Self, has all his holy desires and all the worlds and all joy."[20]

When this Way and End is linked to the doctrines of *karma* and rebirth, then we can see that for the Hindu, this goal may require lifetimes to achieve. But achieve it and realise it we will, since the human is constituted by the Eternal, the Absolute. Thus no matter how caught we are in the *māyā* of ignorance and attachment — the *māyā* that is so dominant within the external life of history through the ages — the flame still burns, however weakly, and will eventually find its way to its proper home.[21]

The *Bhagavad Gītā*, one of the most well-known and popular of Hindu sacred texts, advises that 'we turn Inside, away from the senses' if we are to discover the truth of things.[22] This advice has informed much of Hindu life. It lies as the foundation of meditational practices — which have flourished in abundance over the centuries of the Hindu Way and are spreading in the West in our day — and of ascetic disciplines which seek to tame the senses. But an equally important way to the God within is through devotion, the way of *bhakti*.[23] At least since the fourteenth

18. *Kaṭha Upaniṣad*, p. 66.
19. *Māṇḍūkya Upaniṣad*, p. 78.
20. *Chāndogya Upaniṣad*, p. 126.
21. I am aware that the meaning of *māyā* is much debated within the Hindu Way.
22. *Bhagavad Gītā*, New York: Mentor Books, p. 53.
23. I must acknowledge my debt to Śrīvatsa Goswāmī of Vṛndāban for heightening my awareness of the *bhakti* way. He has welcomed me, often together with my family, into the life of his

→

century, *bhakti* has been the most widely-practiced way within the Hindu Way. And even this way of devotion comes in many forms as is obvious to anyone who has ever travelled across India. Although the way of devotion is practiced throughout the manifold traditions India, one of the most important *bhakti* ways involves devotion to Lord Kṛṣṇa, the *avatāra* of Viṣṇu in the *Gītā*. Kṛṣṇa, in this strand of the Hindu Way, is the divine Beloved who danced his way into the heart of Rādhā and together with Rādhā is the luminous emblem of divine-human love. Here, one encounters the Ultimate as the source, object, and reality of love. One also finds deeply devotional ways in the Śaivite traditions of south India where, daily, temples ring with the songs, drums, cymbals, and dances that embody and effect union with the Beloved Divine. And there is also the important way of *karma-yoga* that emphasises action, but action that is unconditioned by attachment to the results of one's action. Gandhiji is a moving modern Hindu exemplar of this karmic way.[24] The *jñāna-yoga* of Śaṅkarācārya is also widely recognised and admired within Hindu communities, illustrating that these types of *yoga* do not exclude elements of the other *yoga*s. For example, the devotion of Śaṅkara is well-known and supports his *jñāna* way.[25]

The Hindu Way, then, makes its own singular contribution to the human realisation of a spiritual type that transcends the

→ family, the *āśram* of Jai Singh Ghera, the pilgrimage city of Vrindaban and its '10,000 Temples,' to the celebrations in dance of Kṛṣṇa and Rādhā, and to the rituals that mark their religious life.

24. See Gandhi, *An Autobiography: The Story of My Experiments with Truth*, Boston: Beacon Press, 1957 and the biography of Gandhi by L. Fischer, *Gandhi: His Life and Message to the World*, New York: Mentor Books, 1954.

25. See J.G. Arapura, "Śrī Śaṅkarācārya—The Great Philosopher," *Indian Philosophical Annual, 1989-1990*, University of Madras, 1991.

dichotomies that entrap human life. Its secret lies in either in the dancing union of the Self with the Absolute or the realisation that *ātman* (the Self) and *Brahman* (the Absolute) are finally one.

III

THE BUDDHIST WAY: FROM SUFFERING TO ENLIGHTENMENT

From the *Dhammapada*

Arise! Watch
Walk on the right path
He who follows the right path has joy in this world
and in the world beyond.[26]

The Buddhist Way emerges around the life of Siddhārtha Gautama (*c.* 560 BC) — a contemporary of Confucius in China, the prophets of Ancient Israel, the writers of the Upaniṣads in India, the philosophers of Ancient Greece. This time was so spiritually rich that the German philosopher Karl Jaspers called it the 'Axial Period' in recognition of the fact that so much of the spiritual and religious wisdom of humankind emerges in these centuries.[27] The son of a royal family, Siddhārtha abandoned his privileged life in his twenties in response to what legend calls "the Four Passing Sights:" illness, old age, death, and a wandering monk. The first three generated an awareness that life was subject to illness, ageing and death. The fourth suggested another way to be followed. But his path was not easy. He spent six years seeking an answer to his quest. He lived in solitude as a 'forest dweller,' and he practised the austerities of wandering ascetics. Almost despairing of a resolution to his quest, he entered into meditation under the Bo-tree in Bodh Gayā as Siddhārtha and emerged as the Buddha, the Awakened One. He had achieved Enlightenment. He had found the Middle Path.

---

26. *Dhammapada*, 13.168.
27. Karl Jaspers, *The Origin and Goal of History*, New Haven: Yale University Press, 1953, esp., pp. 1-77.

The Buddhist path is encapsulated in the Four Noble Truths and the Eightfold Path. The Four Noble Truths are the insights that (1) life is *duḥkha* (often translated as suffering or sorrow or unsatisfactoriness), (2) the source of *duḥkha* is *tanha* (often translated as craving or selfish desire), (3) there is a way to overcome *tanha* (or forsaking selfish desire leads to the overcoming of suffering), and (4) that way is the Eight-fold Path.[28] These insights are the fruit of Śākyamuni's — to use the preferred Tibetan Buddhist way of naming the historical figure who became the Enlightened One — experience of Enlightenment, when he became the Awakened One, the Buddha. The Eight-fold Path is marked by (1) right view or understanding, (2) right aspiration, (3) right speech, (4) right action, (5) right livelihood, (6) right effort, (7) right mindfulness, (8) right concentration. As this Eight-fold Path has been unfolded in the different streams of Buddhist life — from India across Tibet and China to Korea and Japan, from the island jewel of Sri Lanka to the peoples of south-east Asia — there has been a variety of emphasis and understanding of these different stages and aspects of the journey towards Enlightenment. Though the Englightened One did not himself write anything that remains, his followers compiled a vast literature that has come to be highly revered within Buddhist communities. One of the oldest collections is the so-called Pali Canon of Sri Lanka and Southern Buddhism.[29]

Commitments to the Four Noble Truths and the Eight-fold Path are shared across the streams of Buddhism which include the major division into Theravādin, or the Southern School, and Mahāyāna, or the Northern School. But they have been embroidered on in different ways across the Buddhist world.

---

28. There are many accounts of the Four Noble Truths. See, for example, Francis Story, *Foundations of Buddhism: The Four Noble Truths*, Kandy: Buddhist Publication Society, 1983.
29. See David Kalupahana, *A History of Buddhist Philosophy*, Honolulu: University of Hawaii Press, 1992.

The Sri Lankan Kheminda Thera asserts that "the teaching of the Buddha is in essence the showing forth of the true nature of sentient existence and the proclamation of the path to deliverance from the suffering inherent therein."[30] But others put the emphasis elsewhere. I remember, for example, the beaming face of Han Tap, a Korean Buddhist at Kumsan-sa, as he exclaimed to me, "It is the boundless life, that's Buddhism!"[31] Master Dogen in Japan exclaimed, "Drop mind, drop body."[32] His Holiness Dalai Lama, the Ocean of Wisdom, often reminds his Tibetan community that the Buddhist path is one of compassion.[33] Such differences of emphasis do not overwhelm the core unity across the different schools as their followers seek to become enlightened ones in the path of the Buddha.

The 'boundless life' aspired to in Buddhism is the fruit of a Way and practice that sees human life captive and bound by selfish, craving desire centering around the ego-self. This is the root of our suffering. It revolves around the Buddhist doctrine of *anatta* or 'no soul/no self,' understood as a fixed, eternal substance. As we cling to such a notion, we generate suffering, for all is impermanent and changing. While the goal of the Way — Enlightenment or *nirvāṇa* — exceeds all our descriptions, the Buddha does allow one affirmation: "Bliss, yes bliss, my friends, is *nirvāṇa*."[34] And the

---

30. Kheminda Thera, *The Buddhist Way of Meditation*, Colombo, Sri Lanka: p. 1.
31. I met Han Tap, a Korean Buddhist of the Chogye Order, at Kumsan-sa Monastery, in August of 1992.
32. See Dogen Zenji, *Shobogenzo, The Eye and Treasury of the True Law*, now available in English translation thanks to the remarkable efforts of my friend Kosen Nishiyama, Tokyo: Nakayama Shobo and Japan Publications Trading Co, distributors, 1988.
33. See H.H. the Dalai Lama, *Freedom in Exile*, New York: Harper-Collins, 1990 and *Compassion in Tibetan Buddhism*, tr. by Jeffrey Hopkins, Ithaca, NY: Snow Lion, 1980.
34. Huston Smith, p. 112.

long history of Buddhist reflection and the accounts of followers of the Buddha who became Bodhisattvas or Arhants (the ideal for Mahāyāna and Theravādin, respectively) suggest that such a realisation takes us beyond our ordinary experience of life and, paradoxically, returns us to life with boundless compassion, wonder, bliss. In some streams of Buddhism, it results in the paradoxical affirmation that "*nirvāṇa* is *saṁsāra*, *saṁsāra* is *nirvāṇa*."

Most Buddhist streams of the Buddhist Way emphasise that Enlightenment is the consequence of sustained practice of meditation to overcome the defilements of the mind: greed, lust, and anger. Indeed, many would claim that it is a practice that requires several lifetimes. (I remember meeting a monk who had lived alone for eighteen years and he humbly remarked that he had made 'a little progress' during that time in "overcoming the mind's defilements."[35]) This disciplined meditational practice requires that one assume the role of the monk. The institution of the *Saṁgha* was established in Buddha's own lifetime for those who were 'stream enterers,' or those wholly devoted to the discipline. The *Saṁgha* has persisted to the present day. There were both male and female monks from the very beginning of the Buddhist Way, but some of the female lineages were lost.[36] The lay Buddhist was to support the *Saṁgha*, the monks to teach the *dharma* and all took refuge in the Buddha. Thus evolved patterns of Buddhist society that persist down to the present.

The Buddhist Way offers a *prima facie* 'no' to our thesis that the religious traditions must be seen as 'dialogues with transcendence' given its rejection of the discourse of the God Beyond. But it is clear that the Buddhist goal of Enlightenment,

---

35. See M. Darrol Bryant, "Meeting a Buddhist Monk," *Dialogue and Alliance*, Vol. 2, No. 4, 1988-90, pp. 71-4.

36. See M. D. Bryant, "A Place called Shimwon, A Nun called Cho-ui Sunim," in *Newsletter on International Buddhist Women's Activities*, No. 35, April-June, 1993, pp. 11-13.

the achievement of *nirvāṇa/nibbāna*, is not a mundane reality. It is, in the proper sense, transcendent. As the Enlightened One says:

> There is also, brethren, that which is not born, nor become, nor made. If that were not, there would be no refuge from that which is born, is become, is made. That is the end of sorrow. That is *nirvāṇa*.[37]

Buddhism provides the Way to this end.

Huston Smith remarks,

> Buddhism is a voyage across the river of life, a transport from the common sense shore of non-enlightenment, spiritual ignorance, desire, and death, to the far-flung bank of wisdom which brings liberation from this prevailing bondage.[38]

Thoughout history, it has generated a wide variety of schools and yet the Buddhist Way remains centered on a single aspiration: the achievement of Enlightenment. As the great Japanese interpreter of Buddhism to the West, D.T. Suzuki once remarked, "the opening of *satori* is the remaking of life itself."[39] Or in the words of Christmas Humphreys:

> As the womb and essence of that great system of development known as Buddhism is the Enlightenment of the All-Enlightened One, it follows that in Buddhism the pursuit of enlightenment has supreme priority.[40]

---

37. *Dhammapada*, p. 17. Some streams of Buddhism are more open to the metaphysical discussion than others; see, for example, Keiji Nishitani, *Religion and Nothingness*, Berkeley: University of California Press, 1982. For a fine discussion of faith in the Buddhist Way see Sung Bae Park, *Buddhist Faith and Sudden Enlightenment*, Albany: SUNY Press, 1983.
38. Huston Smith, *The World's Religions*, p. 136.
39. D. T. Suzuki, *Essays in Zen Buddhism*, Vol. I, p. 217.
40. Christmas Humphreys, *The Buddhist Way of Life*, p. 112.

This great Path has shaped the lives of countless human beings throughout the ages. It has given to humankind the image of the serene and compassionate Buddha as the highest calling of humanity.

IV

THE CHRISTIAN WAY: LOVE OF GOD AND THE NEIGHBOUR

From the Book of *Genesis*:

> Come, let us make man in our own image,
> male and female, he created them.[41]

From the Gospel of *John*:

> I came that you might have life,
> and have it abundantly. — *Jn*: 10:10

and

> to those who did accept him
> he gave power to become children of God.[42]

When one encounters the variety of communities that have emerged in the Christian era, it is sometimes hard to remember that the Christian Way emerges around the singular life, death, and resurrection of Jesus of Nazareth.[43] Christians initially regarded Jesus as the Messiah but came to acknowledge him as the Christ, the Divine Logos. In Jesus as the Christ, God is fully present and is revealed as God-with-us in creating, redeeming,

---

41. Genesis 1:1. This text has loomed large in the Christian understanding of marriage. See M. Darrol Bryant, "Marriage in the Christian Tradition: Mystery, Meaning, and Mutuality", forthcoming in *Dialogue and Alliance*, Spring, 1995.

42. John 10:10 and John 1:12.

43. For a fine contemporary study of Jesus, see Marcus Borg, *Jesus: A New Vision*, San Francisco: Harper & Row, 1987.

and sanctifying life.[44] In no other tradition is the Way to the Ultimate so fully linked to a particular divine-human figure. In the Gospel of John, Jesus is identified as the "Way, the Truth and the Life." In Buddhism, it is not so much the person of the Buddha as the message of the Enlightened One that is central.

As the First-Born of a New Creation, the Christ is both archetype of and entrance to a particular spiritual path that leads to union with God. Moreover, the Christian story provides a particular orientation to the whole of our life in time as it unfolds from creation to consummation. Its scriptures tell that story in its mythic narrative from Creation, to Fall, Redemption and Consummation, and it is elaborated in the longer history of Christian thought and reflection. The story of creation, fall, redemption, and consummation is not only a cosmic story, but also a human one. And at the centre of that story stands Jesus as the Christ, the one who restores humanity to the image of God and empowers human beings to become the 'sons and daughters of God.'

The Christian Bible incorporates the scriptures of the Jewish Way plus the writings that came to be known as the New Testament. The letters of Paul are the oldest writings of the New Testament canon, followed by the Gospels. All were written after Jesus' death, some probably as long as seventy years later. Though not direct writings of Jesus, Christians regard them as inspired.[45]

The Christian Way centres on the mediating power and presence of the Risen Christ who redeems humanity and on whom is bestowed the gift of the Holy Spirit. The follower of

---

44. Of my essays on the Trinity, see especially, "Interfaith Encounter and Dialogue in a Trinitarian Perspective," in Peter Phan, (ed.), *Christianity and the Wider Ecumenism*, New York: Paragon House, 1990, pp. 3-20.

45. The long-standing doctrine of the Bible as the "inspired Word of God" has come under attack in recent centuries.

Christ is one who is made one with God in the transforming power of faith and is called to live a life of sacrificial love. Jesus summed up his message in the Gospels as "love God and the Neighbour."

Immediately following Jesus' death at the hands of Roman authorities and his mysterious Resurrection, the Christian Way gave rise to a *koinonia* or community. Those communities of Christian believers were planted by the early disciples and apostles throughout the ancient world, by Paul in Rome and Thomas in India.[46] They developed ritual forms, but especially central were those of baptism and the eucharist. Baptism signaled entrance into the community. The eucharist is the communal meal that both remembers Jesus' life and death and anticipates the fulfilment of the reign of God. Those communities also developed hierarchical structures that have come to permeate the Christian Way over the centuries. Christians came to belong to one of three major divisions within the Christian Way: Roman Catholic, Orthodox, and Protestant. Within the Protestant traditions one finds, literally, hundreds of different denominations. The ecumenical movement of the twentieth century has begun to awaken the Christian world to an awareness of a shared unity that is greater than the historic differences that gave rise to all the divisions within Christianity.

Thomas a Kempis, a medieval mystic, emphasised that the Christian life was an '*imitatio Christi*,' the imitation of Christ.[47] But this is not to be understood in a slavish way but rather that the Christ as perfect humanity is the gateway to the fullness of humanity that God seeks for all. For we are called, in the Christian Way, to reenact Christ's life as life-unto-God. The

46. See W.H.C. Frend, *The Rise of Christianity*, Philadelphia: Fortress Press, 1984. Two sabbaticals in India have left me more open to the legend of Thomas in India.

47. Thomas a'Kempis, *The Imitation of Christ*, is a popular Christian text from the late middle ages.

unity of Christ with God means that Christ opens a way to God wherein we become the sons and daughters of that One in whose image humanity was made. The obstacle to that humanity is sin, the breaking of the divine-human relationship. It is sin which disorders human life in myriad ways and leads humanity to become something less than God intended. It is the Christ that restores that relationship between God and Humanity thus making Christ, in Irenaeus's words, 'the first-born of a new humanity.'

The Christian Way emphasises the centrality of faith. Faith should not to be confused with believing absurd things but as the power which can reorient the deeper Self towards God. In the New Testament, faith is the experience of *metanoia*, being turned around. With that experience of metanoia, the human journey can then unfold towards its proper divine end and exhibits a life transformed by redeeming love that is exemplified in love of the neighbour. It is in the Jesus who broke bread with sinners, always lived responsive to the will of God, and was raised by God that we have an image of human life fulfilled.

Within the Christian Way, there are those who understand the Way primarily in ontological terms — it is the break in the relationship between God and Humanity that must be restored — and those who understand the Way in primarily ethical terms — the Christian is one who follows the teaching of Jesus. And still others understand the Christian Way in primarily ritual and sacramental terms. All, however, place the Christ at the heart of the Way and agree that to become more Christ-like is the heart of the Christian Way.[49]

It is this Christian Way that opens up a spiritual type that contributes to the making of humanity in relation to the Ultimate: becoming the sons and daughters of God, the Divine Ground.

---

49. See, for example, John Cobb, *The Structure of Christian Existence*, Philadelphia: Westminster Press, 1967.

V

THE MUSLIM WAY: SURRENDER AS FULFILMENT

The Way of Islam, the peace that comes from surrender to Allāh, was born out of the profound revelation to the Prophet Muhammed of Allāh, "the Gracious, the Merciful, the Beneficent."[50] Born in AD 571, Muhammad was early orphaned. He entered the caravan business of a wealthy widow named Khadija. They were married, and fifteen years later, following deep prayer and meditation, Muhammad began to receive revelation from Allāh. Initially terrified, he came to submit and thus received the *Korān*. Central to Muhammad's experience and his recognition as the Prophet of Allāh was the gift of the *Korān*, the sacred text of the Muslim Way. As a gift of Allāh, it is regarded by the faithful Muslim as "God's message to humankind." It announces that there is no God but God, or Allāh in Arabic. Muslims also speak of the 'ninety-nine names of God,' names that point to God's perfections or attributes, like Rahman (most Gracious) and Rahīm (most Merciful). The *Korān* not only gives us this name of God and seeks to recall us to remembrance of the Creator, but also provides direction for human social life. For the Muslim, one can move directly from the divine direction given in the *Korān* to life-together in society.[51]

The Muslim Way is encapsulated in what are known as the

---

50. I must acknowledge that the family of Dr. Syyed Ausaf Ali and Naheed, together with their daughters Leena and Muna, are never far from my thoughts when I think of this living faith. Ever since our first meeting in the early 1980s, they have played a crucial role in my learning of the Muslim Way. They have been a second family to our family while on sabbatical in India in 1986-7 and again in 1993-4. I am immensely grateful to them in every way. They welcomed our family into their life in New Delhi with remarkable warmth and generosity.

51. See S. Murata & W. C. Chittick, *The Vision of Islam*, New York: Paragon House, 1995.

Five Pillars. The first pillar of the Islamic Way is the affirmation, "There is no God but Allāh and Muhammad is His Prophet." It is often called the Islamic Creed. The second pillar is a life of prayer. Specifically, Muslims are enjoined to pray five times daily: upon rising, at noon, in the mid-afternoon, after sunset and before retiring. Wherever you find Muslims, you will hear the beautiful early morning call to prayer just before dawn. It is a call to all believers to remember the Creator, the Gracious, the Merciful, and thus the prayer begins: "Allāhu Akbar, God is most great." The prayer most often recited is the opening Surāh of the *Korān*, which begins as follows:

> Praise belongs to Allāh, Lord of the Worlds,
> The Compassionate, the Merciful,
> King of the Day of Judgement.
> 'Tis Thee we worship and Thee we ask for help.
> Guide us in the straight path. . . .[52]

The third pillar of Islam is charity or alms. All Muslims are required to share their material goods with the poor. An annual tax of 2-1/2 per cent was early on instituted within the Muslim world to assist those in need. The fourth pillar is the observance of Ramadān, a lunar month of fasting during the daylight hours. Neither food nor drink passes the lips of the devout Muslim during daylight of this sacred month. The fifth pillar is the pilgrimage to Meccā. Muslims are encouraged to make a pilgrimage to Meccā, if at all possible, the holiest site in the Muslim tradition. These disciplines, like spiritual disciplines in other traditions, seek to conform the believer to the Transcendent. At the same time, they have an obvious human side as they form

52. This is the Opening Surah of the *Korān*. For English translations of the *Korān*, see M.M. Pickthall, (tr.), *The Meaning of the Glorious Koran*, New York: Mentor Books, 1953; A.Y. Ali, tr. and commentary, *The Holy Qur'an*, Brentwood, MD: Amana Corp., 1989; and Rafiq Zakaria, *Muhammad and the Quran*, New Delhi: Penquin Books, 1991, which includes large translated selections from the *Korān*.

humanity in a particular way, in the Muslim way.

The Muslim way centres upon Allāh, the Gracious, the Merciful, the Beneficent. It is the encounter with the Transcendent as it was mediated to Muhammad that is the heart of the spiritual path given in Islam. Often characterised as intolerant of other ways, the *Korān* itself declares that there is 'no people to whom Allāh has not given a prophet.'[53] Islam respects the many Prophets of God — from Noah to Abrāham to Īsā — but Muslims believe that Muhammad is 'the Seal of the Prophets.' Some Muslims understand this to mean that what is announced to Muhammad confirms and completes the story of God's revelation to humanity; others understand it to mean that after Muhammad, there will be no further prophets of God.

The *Korān* was given to the Prophet over a twenty-three-year period. But as soon as Muhammad became convinced of the Truth given to him, he began to share this message with others and to form a community. First in Medinā, then in Meccā, there emerged a vital faith and community that spread across all of Arabia by the time of his death in 10 AH (AD 632). This faith continued to spread so that within a century after his death, it had stretched from North Africa across the Middle East to ancient Persia.

But within a generation after Muhammad's death, a major division took place within the Islamic community. The two streams of Islam became known as Sunnī and Shiite, and both persist to the present day. The mystical path also flourished within Islam and came to be known as the Sūfī way. Sūfī

---

53. *Korān* 16:36. See also Badru Dungu Kateregga, "Islam in Dialogue with People of Faith — Insights from the Islamic Tradition," pp. 109-18 in M.D. Bryant & F.K. Flinn, *Interreligious Dialogue: Voices from a New Frontier*, New York: Paragon House, 1989. For an exceptional work on the feminine in Islam see Sachiko Murata, *The Tao of Islam*, Albany: SUNY Press, 1992.

Muslims, for example, understand the *jihād* (holy war) in spiritual terms: it is the war fought within the human heart as it struggles to submit.[54]

Within the Muslim way, humanity prior to Allāh's revelation to the Prophet was characterised by a forgetfulness of the Creator that led to confusion, disorientation, and immorality. Islam is the antidote to this condition. Some Muslim writers see the heart of the Islamic way in the notion of *Tawhīd*. Muhammad Nejatullah Siddiqi, for example, defines *tawhīd* as

> . . . the essence of being human . . . the restoration of human dignity. . . . what Allāh desires of man [humanity] becomes value for him, the end of human endeavour. One who commits himself to the will of Allāh recognises no authority except His and accepts no guidance other than His. This commitment is total as well as positive and vigorous. It involves love and worship, obedience and submission combined with an eagerness to do His Will and the sense of a mission.[55]

It is this Way that lies at the heart of Islam in its making of the spiritual type that is exemplified in the Prophet Muhammad (Peace be upon him). Siddiqi's description also points to the character of Islamic faith as wholly centered in Allāh. It is an

---

54. See my "Meeting at Snowmass: Some Dynamics of an Interfaith Encounter," pp. 1-20 in John Miller, *Interfaith Dialogue, Four Studies*, Waterloo, ON: University of Waterloo Press, 1986. It describes an interfaith gathering and includes a Sūfī, Imam Hyde, speaking about '*jihād*' (11-12). See also Syed H. Nasr, *Sufi Essays*, London: G. Allen & Unwin, 1972. Nasr's writings have been immensely important in interpreting Islam to the world.

55. Muhammad Nejatullah Siddiqi, 'Tawhīd,' pp. 17-34 in Khurshid Ahmad and Zafar Ishaq Ansari (eds.), *Islamic Perspectives*, London: The Islamic Foundation & The Saudi Publishing House, Jeddah, 1979, p. 17.

instructive observation, for each path to the Ultimate, not just Islam, sees itself as having received the fullness of the Transcendent. It seems to be a characteristic of the classical Ways that their experience of the Absolute is so overwhelming and complete that it seems to exhaust the ineffable Transcendent.

For the Islamic Way, Allāh is the Creator of the Universe and at the heart of creation stands the human as God's 'vice-regent.' It is humanity that is to assume responsibility for itself and the creation. Humanity is free to submit to Allāh and assume this heavenly responsibility with the guidance of the Holy *Korān*. Humanity will also be held accountable for what we as individuals, and as one humanity, have done with the life that has been given to us. We are free, but we are also liable to the judgement which stands over the whole of humanity. These theological convictions stand behind the Way given in Islam, a Way which centers not on belief but on life lived in conformity to God's revelation in the *Korān*. It is a remarkable Way that now encompasses over one-quarter of the human race.[56]

VI

THE CONFUCIAN WAY: HARMONIOUS RELATIONS

Let me place over this brief account of the Confucian Way a well-known summary of that Way:

> If there be righteousness in the heart,
> there will be beauty in the character.
> If there be beauty in the character,
> there will be harmony in the home.
> If there be harmony in the home,

56. See Ismail and Lois al Faruqi, *The Cultural Atlas of Islam*, New York: Macmillan, 1986 and D.L. & J.T. Carmody, *In the Path of the Masters, Understanding the Spirituality of Buddha, Confucius, Jesus, & Muhammad*, New York: Paragon, 1994.

See also, M. Darrol Bryant and S.A. Ali, *Muslim — Christian Dialogue: Promise and Problems*, St. Paul, MN: Paragon, 1998.

there will be order in the nation.
If there be order in the nation,
there will be peace in the world.[57]

And from the *Analects*,

> Heaven has appointed me to teach this doctrine,
> and until I do, what can the people of Kwang do to me?[58]

The Confucian Way emerged in ancient China around one known as the Teacher, Master Kung (*c.* 550 BC). He gave in his teaching a Way that has profoundly shaped the life of humanity in China. It is not characterised by a strong transcendental element, but transcendence is nevertheless present.[59] Symbolised as the Golden Past and the Mandate of Heaven, transcendence is the touchstone of Confucius' teaching. For Confucius, humanity is regarded in essentially social terms. The major issue is to structure human life together in ways that generate social harmony as well as harmony with the Heavenly Mandate.

The Confucian way revolves around the human qualities of *jen* (or human-heartedness) and *chun-tzu* (or true humanity) and the Five Relationships. The Confucian discussion of *jen*, composed, Huston Smith notes, of the Chinese characters for 'man' and 'two' and perhaps best translated as human-heartedness, is instructive.[60] For when the notion of human heartedness is unfolded and linked to *chun-tzu*, it turns out to have the character of the Confucian ideal for humanity, the person of propriety. One discovers something similar in other

---

57. From *The Great Learning* as quoted in Huston Smith, *The World's Religions*, p. 160.
58. *Analects*, IX.5.
59. See Huston Smith, "Transcendence in Traditional China," *Huston Smith: Essays on World Religion*, M. Darrol Bryant (ed.), New York: Paragon House, 1992, pp. 57-70.
60. See Huston Smith, *The World's Religions*, p. 172.

traditions as well. It turns out that discussions of humanity are circular: the notion of humanity is understood in the very terms of the tradition within which the question is articulated. To mention but three examples: in the Christian tradition, it is Christ that exemplifies the fullness of humanity; in Buddhism, it is the Buddha; in Islam, it is Muhammed who is the perfect example of one who submits. Likewise, in the Confucian tradition, the very notion of *jen* or human-heartedness receives it image and understanding from the Confucian ideal of *chun tzu*, which is exemplified in Confucius himself. In other words, the very notion of humanity does not remain general and empty but is given content by the specific tradition itself.[61]

For the Confucian Way, the human problem is not occasioned by suffering, as in Buddhism, or by an ontological break in the relationship of God and humanity, as in Christianity. Rather, the human problem is social; it has to do with the relationships between human beings. Humanity is not ontologically flawed but is in need of sound instructions so that we can live in harmony with one another and Heaven's Way.

The social focus of the Confucian way is exemplified in its focus on 'the Five Relationships.' Those are the relationships between (a) father and son, (b) elder brother and junior brother, (c) husband and wife, (d) elder friend and junior friend, and (e) ruler and subject. It is clear that the family, the focus of three of the five relationships, is fundamental to the Confucian vision. It is in the family that we have the basic social unit, and as relations within the family unfold properly, we have the basis for social harmony.

---

61. For an impressive discussion of the Confucian Way see Tu Wei-Ming, *Confucian Thought, Selfhood as Creative Transformations*, Albany: SUNY Press, 1985, especially "The Value of the Human in Classical Confucian Thought," pp. 67-80. For a comparative discussion of humanity, including the Confucian Way see D.L. & J.T. Carmody, *In the Path of the Masters*, pp. 41-4, 76-8, 115-18, and 152-6.

Of almost equal importance in Confucianism is the ritual side of *li* or propriety. Many in the West, largely under the impact of the Protestant heritage, tend to disparage ritual as empty form. But the Confucian sees rites as the way to maintain the harmony between heaven and earth and among all things on the earth. Thus there is often a ritual character to human relations in the Confucian Way as well as rites *per se*. Perhaps the central rite for the Confucian is in relation to the ancestors, the dead. The Western philosopher Burke once described society as "the living, the dead, and the yet unborn." Confucius would agree. And ritual is the way to maintain the proper relationship between the dead, the ancestors, and the living. Reverence for the ancestors is not to be confused with 'ancestor worship.' It is the way of maintaining a proper relationship with those who preceded us. As we recall and remember them, we are reinstructed in the moral virtues and harmony between the living and dead is maintained.[62] After Confucius' own time, there also came to be elaborate state rituals to maintain the proper relations between the earthly and heavenly spheres. Rites are important to the Confucian Way since they establish proper relations between things both in the heavenly realm and in the earthly.

The Confucian Way addresses itself to the issue of proper social relationships that can move humanity towards harmonious life. The Confucian spiritual archetype, Confucius said, was not perfected in any human being; but for Confucians, it was exemplified in Confucius himself. He had given his life to goodness (*jen*), true humanity (*chun tzu*), propriety (*li*), government by virtue (*te*), and the arts of peace (*wen*). Though not himself successful in attaining a political position that would enable him to effect his teaching, he none the less was able to profoundly shape the life of the Chinese and other East Asian

62. See the Thematic Issue of the *Journal of the AAR*, "Studies in Classical Chinese Thought," Vol. XLVII, No. 3, September, 1979.

peoples. His teachings were gathered into the *Analects* by his disciples after his death in 479 BC. He became for the Chinese **the** Master whose Way was to shape Chinese life down to the present century.

VII

THE SIKH WAY: ECSTASY AND SEVĀ

From the *Śrī Guru Granth Sāhib*,

> Innumerable the forms of devotion.
> Innumerable the forms of worship . . .
> Innumerable are God's names . . .[63]

And

> The Lord Supreme is all dieties
> He is Śiva, Viṣṇu, Brahman
> And the Goddesses Pārbatī, Lakṣamī, and Sarasvatī
> Here I realise His true greatness,
> How may I utter it?[64]

The Sikh Way emerges around the life of Guru Nānak (1469-

---

63. The Sikh scriptures are called the *Ādi Granth* or *Guru Granth* or *Guru Granth Sāhib*. They are the only world scripture, to my knowledge, to be composed wholly of songs of praise. For a discussion of the *Guru Granth Sāhib*, see W. Owen Cole and Piara Singh Sambhi, *The Sikhs, Their Religious Beliefs and Practices*, London: Routledge & Kegan Paul, 1978, pp. 43-57 and G.S. Talib, *An Introduction to Guru Granth Sahib*, Patiala: Publication Bureau of the Punjabi University, 1991. The specific text is from pp. I.9-10, *Śrī Guru Granth Sāhib*, tr. by G. S. Talib, 3 Vols., Patiala: Punjabi University, 1984-7. For an interpretation of the Sikh tradition in relation to the contemporary dialogue of religions, see M. Darrol Bryant, "The Sikh Tradition and Dialogue or Why Sikhs are Open to Dialogue," *The Guru Gobind Singh Journal of Religious Studies*, Vol. 1, 1994, pp. 6-23.
64. *Śrī Guru Granth*, tr. by Talib, p. I.4.

1539) and the nine succeeding *gurus*. The tradition of a living human *guru* came to an end with the tenth *guru*, Guru Gobind Singh (1675-1708), who installed the *Guru Granth Sāhib* — the Sikh scripture — as the 'living *guru*' of the Sikh tradition. It seems important to include this more recent religious tradition in order to underscore the fact that new religious ways continue to emerge. Moreover, it allows us to see that though there are elements in the Sikh Way that are shared with other traditions, both Hindu and Muslim,[65] it is none the less a distinctive way and creates a distinctive human type: the ecstatic disciple. Sikh means literally 'disciple' or 'follower.'

Born of Hindu parents and employed by a Muslim official, Nānak's life was changed by a profound experience near the age of thirty. He had long practised the religious life and led the community in singing hymns of praise to God when he went for his morning ablutions. But one day, he didn't return home and he was missing for three days. Many presumed he had drowned. When he reappeared, he was silent except for a simple but enigmatic statement: 'There is no Hindu, there is no Muslim.' Some stories of this event recount Nānak going on to say, "So whose path shall I follow? I shall follow God's path. God is neither Hindu, nor Muslim." It was later sung that Nānak had been transported to the Heavenly Courts where he had been given a vocation "to become God's minstrel, to sing God's praise."[66] For Nānak, God exceeded the divisions of Hindu and Muslim; God was more than could be contained in the designations of Hindu or Muslim. For the next years, he wandered across India and beyond in conversation with saints and holy men wherever

65. Their is considerable controversy raging around the issue of the 'uniqueness' of the Sikh tradition. See, for example, K. Singh, G.S. Mansukhani, J.S. Mann (eds.), *Fundamental Issues in Sikh Studies*, a publication of the Institute of Sikh Studies, Chandigarh, 1992.

66. See O. Cole and P. Sambhi, *The Sikhs*, *op.cit.*, pp. 8ff.

he encountered them, always singing of the one Beyond, *Ek Oṁkār*. When he was fifty, he settled in Kartārpur but continued his vocation as God's minstrel.

Guru Nānak was to be the first of a series of ten living *gurus*. The tenth was Guru Gobind Singh (d. *c*.1708) who announced that he was the last of the living *gurus* and that from henceforth the *Śrī Guru Granth Sāhib*, the Sikh Scripture, was to be regarded as the Living *guru*. The Sikh scripture is, to my knowledge, unique in the history of religions: it is composed entirely of hymns that are to be sung. It includes hymns from six of the Sikh *gurus*. But it is striking in the fact that it contains many hymns that are from 'non-Sikhs,' in the narrow historical sense. It includes hymns by figures like Kabīr, the poet-weaver of Benāres, by Shaikh Farīd, a Muslim *pīr*, and by Rām Dās, a Hindu *bhakta*. These hymns exemplify the conviction that the Eternal God exceeds our historic forms, our diverse symbols, our many divisions. It is that One that, in the Sikh Way, we are called to praise.

Yet the Sikh Way came too to be identified with particular symbols and particular communities. Following Guru Gobind Singh, that central community became the Khālsā Sikhs marked by the Five *kakkars* or 'Ks': *keśa* or uncut hair, *kaṁghā* or the wooden or ivory comb, *kirpān* or the ceremonial sword, *karā* or the simple steel bracelet, and *kacchā* or short undergarment. These were the marks of the historic community that had partaken of the holy *amṛt* (initiation into the *Kalaśa*) and engaged in a life of service, called *sevā*. Within the Sikh community today, there is a lively debate concerning these marks of particularity. That discussion reflects a perennial problem that faces religious communities: the way to embody the path to the Transcendent God in a particular community in time.[67]

---

67. This is a lively issue within contemporary Sikhism. See the story of Gobind Sadan by Mary Pat Fisher, *Everyday Miracles in the House of God*, New Delhi: Gobind Sadan, 1992.

These universal elements are reflected in the fact that the community eschewed caste and affirmed the equality of all in relation to God and to one another. The tradition of the *langar*, or common meal, served daily in the Sikh Gurdvārā (place of worship), pointed to this equality and the tradition of service. It also embodies their shared status as Sikhs and their recognition of all humanity as seekers and disciples of the Divine *guru*. It has been a Way that has enriched life as it seeks to conform the disciple — through meditation, the sung hymns of the *Guru Granth*, the rites of the Gurdvārā, and a life of labour in the world — to the God Above all religious divisions.

VIII

MAKING HUMANITY IN THE CRUCIBLE OF TRANSCENDENCE

The Glory of God in Polyphonic Humanity

In this brief presentation of the Hindu, Buddhist, Christian, Islamic, Confucian and Sikh Ways to the Ultimate, we have sought to see each in its own terms while pointing to the spiritual type that lies at the heart of each tradition. We have tried to suggest that each tradition aims at forming our polyphonic humanity in the image of its fundamental encounter with and experience of the Ultimate. At the same time, there are some things shared across tradition. For example, each of these Ways to the Ultimate involves an encounter with Transcendence in a three-fold way. First, it involves an encounter with Transcendence understood as the divine ground and end/goal of all things. I realise that this way of putting the matter can be misleading in relation to the Buddhist tradition with its emphasis on 'Emptiness.'[68] But here the notion of Transcendence is not to be restricted to the theistic traditions. Secondly, it is an encounter

68. This is more problematic in some schools of Buddhism than others. See for example the works of the Kyoto school cited above which are more amenible to this metaphysical account.

with Transcendence as a Way. As Ways, the religious traditions are diverse, different. Yet each Way facilitates the transcendence of those bonds of human disorder. That disorder is identified in particular ways — as ignorance in Hinduism, as grasping in Buddhism, as sin in Christianity, as forgetfulness in Islam — that keep humanity from attaining that fullness of humanity that we are destined to attain. Thirdly, as **spiritual** paths, they transcend the mundane, opening possibilities that would otherwise remain closed to human unfolding and the making of humankind. Yet it is precisely in the world of space-time that these spiritual types are to be realised. They enable the human to realise itself at the deepest level, that place where the mundane is transcended and the divinely-human or humanly-divine is attained. For the religious traditions, it is the destiny of humanity to be related to the Ultimate. And the pathways of the different religious traditions are simultaneously the Ways to the Ultimate and to the multiform making of multiform humanity.

4

A Grammar of the Spirit

Making Humanity in Persons, Society and History

Without destiny there would only be females and males, yellow men and black men, Bostonians and Los Angelenos, eternally divided. But these are the sons and daughters of the One Man. A common destiny for all children of man has been achieved for us.[1]

In this lecture, I want to turn our attention from the understanding of dialogical humanity in the crucible of Transcendence and the multiform religious pathways to the Ultimate to an important example of the attempt to see the centrality of the Spirit across the whole of human intergenerational and historical life. Again, my guide in this exploration will be the work of Eugen Rosenstock-Huessy as I have interpreted his insights and extended them beyond the contexts ofhis writings. Though Rosenstock-Huessy was shaped by Western Christian culture and history, he was gifted with an openness to the achievements of the whole of human cultural and religious life. Moreover, his account ofhuman unfolding has parallels in the four stages of life in the Hindu traditions and with the Buddhist charting of the eight-fold path that divides

---

1. Eugen Rosenstock-Huessy, *Planetary Service*, p. xvii. The whole effort of these lectures could be seen as a gloss on Acts 17:28, "In him we live and move and have our being."

that path into the stages of moral growth, serenity formation, and wisdom/compassion.[2]

Rosenstock-Huessy provides an important example of understanding the human story as it unfolds in relation to a destiny that ever exceeds us, for that destiny rests within the Unmanifest Ultimate itself. Rosenstock-Huessy's work is an example of what I earlier referred to a 'grammar of the spirit' found within the different religious traditions.

Our point of departure is a little essay by Rosenstock-Huessy entitled "The Twelve Tones of the Spirit".[3] In this essay, Rosenstock-Huessy continued his relentless quest to discern — and articulate — the presence of the Spirit in the life of humankind in time. Here, he focused his attention on the stages of a human life as what he called childhood, adulthood, and elderhood. These stages have parallels with the Hindu stages of student, householder, retirement, and *saṁnyāsin*. Within each of these stages, he identifies four distinctive 'tones of the Spirit' that make for the fullness of life stretching from birth to death. Thus there emerge twelve tones of the Spirit that are correlated with these three stages or phases of a human life. Within each of these phases, we, as particular human beings and as part of the intergenerational fabric of a society, are called to enact a series of notes crucial to attaining the fullness of life. As youth, Rosenstock-Huessy contends, we are called 'to obey, read, learn, sing;' as adults "to doubt and withhold, analyse and synthesise, speak up and insist, wait and persevere;" and as elders "to lead and legislate, teach and instruct, prophesy and warn, endow and

---

2. See, for example, the discussion of a Buddhist 'grammar' in Mahasi Sayadaw, *Practical Insight Meditation: Basic and Progressive Stages*, Kandy: Buddhist Publication Society, 1971.

3. Eugen Rosenstock-Huessy, "The Twelve Tones of the Spirit," in *I am an Impure Thinker*, Norwich, VT: Argo Books, 1970, pp. 69-78.

bestow."[4] These activities, Rosenstock-Huessy writes, are "the way by which we are threaded into God's creation, day after day, that is into his history. . . ."[5]

What is striking here is Rosenstock-Huessy's conviction that the story of a human life is not a mere unfolding of a biological given or a series of movements in a process of socialisation, but rather a dramatic unfolding of the life of the Spirit in the narrative of the divine economy that stretches from its destiny in the Ultimate to its beginnings in the Beyond, or, as he stunningly argues, from the End to the Beginning. For Rosenstock-Huessy, the life of the Spirit in time, this narrative of human destiny, is lived backwards: from the consummation towards creation, from death to birth. And thus, as he says, "creation is taking place under our very noses."[6] Creation is not, in this perspective, an event in some distant past but a continuing dimension of our life in time as we are being made fit for the Ultimate, as we move towards our divine destiny.

It is my intention here to attempt to unfold this 'grammar of the spirit' and to relate it to the theme of these lectures: the many faiths and the "one developing purpose running through the ages." But in order to move towards that end, it will be necessary to recall some of the larger themes of Rosenstock-Huessy's work in order to grasp this 'grammar of the spirit.' The assumption — one I hope to demonstrate here — is that there is a structural or morphological identity to the Spirit in the writings of Rosenstock-Huessy, whether we are looking at history or the inter-generational life of particular human beings or humanity as a whole. What varies is the scale and complexity, or better, the multiformity, of the human order that Rosenstock-Huessy sought to grasp. While his particular understanding of the patterns of

---

4. Rosenstock-Huessy, "Twelve Tones . . . ," p. 74.
5. *Ibid.*, p. 71.
6. *Ibid.*, pp. 70-1.

the Spirit in time is inspired by his Christian faith, it is my conviction that such patterns are to be found in all the great traditions. The clues to those patterns are present in the mythic narratives that are found within the different traditions. One could, for example, imagine a Buddhist account that begins with Enlightenment as the ultimate end of humanity and then reads the human story in time from the perspective of that fundamental intuition of human destiny.[7]

When Rosenstock-Huessy reads history, he reads it from the end to the beginning; when he describes a culture, it is from the end back. Or, in the language we have used here, he reads history from the perspective of humankind's destiny: the creation of humankind in the singular, a destiny that is fulfilled in the Ultimate itself.[8] The reason for this is, finally, simple: the Spirit, which is the presence of the Ultimate in life, is stronger than death. It is the destiny that awaits the whole of humanity.

But to say that this is simple is to speak from within the circle of faith that Rosenstock-Huessy assumes in all his writing. Within that Christian expression of the circle, the great secret is that 'death precedes life.' In other religious traditions, that insight would be expressed in other terms, terms appropriate to each tradition's own vision of the Ultimate. But to those outside those circles, those who fail to acknowledge the Spirit, this view is sheer nonsense. Nevertheless, as Rosenstock-Huessy sought repeatedly to demonstrate, this truth is given in life itself. Hence it is more by attending to the dynamics of life than by attending

---

7. See the story of Tibetan History, cited above, for another example. One could also look at *The Mahavamsa or The Great Chronicle of Ceylon*, tr. by W. Geiger, Colombo: Ceylon Government Information Department, 1950.

8. See my "Toward a Grammar of the Spirit in Society," pp. 173-90 in M.D. Bryant & R.H. Mataragnon, *The Many Faces of Religion and Society*, New York: Paragon House, 1985, especially pp. 178ff.

to a Christianity that has lost its own grasp of this truth that we can hear the tones of the Spirit that pervade human life and lift it into 'his history,' divine history.[9]

II

In the '*Twelve Tones of the Spirit*,' we hear echoes of a theme that permeates Rosenstock-Huessy's writings. That theme is stated in various ways but centres on "the task of revealing God in society", or what we, following Eugen Rosenstock-Huessy, are calling here 'the making of humankind.'[10] These are not two themes, but one interrelated theme, since for Rosenstock-Huessy, it is in the making of humankind that God is disclosed. That task focuses on the Spirit, the Third article of the Christian Creed, but, as he says, 'the first article of our experience.'[11] It is in our experience, from childhood through adulthood to elderhood, that we encounter the twelve tones of the spirit. Let me quote him at length:

> You know as well as I that the Spirit permeates our carnal bodies in at least three steps: He enters into us. This stage is called childhood. Everything, in this phase, is received by the child with the zest of 'first-ness;' 'new'

---

9. See M.D. Bryant & Hans Huessy (eds.), *Eugen Rosenstock-Huessy: Studies in his Life and Thought*, *op.cit*.

10. This way of seeing the human story as a making of humanity is found throughout Rosenstock-Huessy's writings. See Eugen Rosenstock-Huessy, "In Defense of the Grammatical Method," *Speech and Reality*, Norwich, VT: Argo Books, 1970, where he defines the task of social analysis as "the search for the omnipresence of God in the most contradictory patterns of human society," p. 42. Or, Eugen Rosenstock-Huessy, *The Christian Future, Or the Modern Mind Outrun*, New York: Harper & Row, 1966, where he speaks about 'anthropurgy' or the 'making of humankind' pp. 108 ff.

11. Rosenstock-Huessy, "Twelve Tones . . . ," p. 71.

> equals 'inspiration,' during childhood.
>
> Then, however, this spirit begins to work in us. He stirs us up. He abides in us and transforms us. This phase we may call adulthood. Lastly, the Spirit being a power cannot be secluded inside of us. He holds forth, he proceeds outside. This stage we may call elderhood, or with the Greek corresponding term, priesthood.[12]

Here, clearly, Rosenstock-Huessy declares his opposition to 'naturalism,' that is, the view that the human story can be accounted for without reference to the spiritual, and to 'secularism,' which Rosenstock-Huessy here identifies as reversing the spiritual order by assuming that the child "should pull itself up by its own bootstraps and become itself, express itself, live by itself."[13] Rather, for Rosenstock-Huessy, "the Spirit permeates our carnal bodies." Hence we are a more complex being than can be measured only by reference to biological mechanisms or by counting. To get the human story right, we must recognise the presence of the Spirit at the very beginning. But this Spirit — and here Rosenstock-Huessy stands in opposition to that body/spirit dualism that has so bedeviled Christianity — is present, as it were, to the very life of the body.

Thus the human person stands at the intersection of a two-fold process: on the biological front, one is proceeding from birth to death, but on the spiritual front, the reverse is occurring. The spiritual tone thus transforms the biological moment and brings it to its fullness in the intergenerational context of society. The moment the child is born, he or she is in an intergenerational context where the twelfth tone of the spirit — to heed or obey — is linked, across generations, with the elders' first tone of testator. It is the word spoken across generations that lifts the

---

12. Rosenstock-Huessy, "Twelve Tones . . . ," p. 71.

13. *Ibid.*, p. 73.

child beyond itself into the society of generations and thus adds a dimension of the spirit to the bodily. Although it is somewhat awkward to list Rosenstock-Huessy's twelve tones of the spirit here, such a list might clarify this point:[14]

	Bodily		Spiritually
		Childhood	
	1	obey	12
I	2	read	11
N	3	learn	10
T	4	sing	9
E			
R			
		Adulthood	
G			
E	5	doubt and withhold	8
N	6	analyse and synthesise	7
E	7	speak up and insist	6
R	8	wait and persevere	5
A			
T		**Elderhood**	
I			
O	9	lead and legislate	4
N	10	teach and instruct	3
A	11	prophesy and warn	2
L	12	endow and bestow	1

Not only does one find oneself at the intersection of the twelve

14. Rosenstock-Huessy, "Twelve Tones . . . ," p. 74.

tones of the spirit with the body, but also in the midst of generations. Thus there is, as Rosenstock-Huessy acknowledges, a sense in which all of the tones are present at each stage, but "each tone should be given one period of life for its fullest cultivation."[15] Moreover, it is the cultivating of each tone that prepares the child to achieve the rhythm that constitutes our intergenerational life and growth in the Spirit. The failure, for example, to obey, Rosenstock-Huessy argues, precludes a later ability to command. This is analogous to the reciprocity between speaking and hearing that pervades Rosenstock-Huessy's writings: the person who can never hear another cannot grasp the power of speaking, nor can his/her speech be more than empty chatter. Likewise, Rosenstock-Huessy observes that the stage of testator is preceded by eleven earlier stages which give substance, depth and meaning to his testimony.

Perhaps one illustration of this two-fold process or intertwining of the spirit and the body might be helpful. Let me choose an example that has bedeviled and often confused the religious traditions themselves. Our example concerns human sexuality, specifically in relation to adolescence and the dawning of 'genital sexuality' in young people. Somewhere — but I can't recall the specific reference — Rosenstock-Huessy speaks of this two-fold process in relation to puberty. Here, he reminds us that the biological process of sexual maturation is linked to a spiritual purpose: the preparation for a new kind of love relationship with persons of the opposite sex. It is not just a biological process but at the same time a call or tone of the spirit that ushers us into a new form of human community. Now the young person is not only son or daughter in relation to the parents, but is also preparing for the relationship of lover/loved with a member of the opposite sex. Presumably, the child has passed through the earlier stages of auto and homo-sexuality and is capable both biologically and spiritually of a form of sexuality that is able to

15. Rosenstock-Huessy, "Twelve Tones . . . ," p. 74.

relate to the other as 'other,' i.e., heterosexuality. The point is that the failure to recognise the spiritual calling that is coterminous with the biological shift and development can easily lead to confusion or distortion if it is understood only in biological or naturalistic terms. But when it is linked to this one of the spirit, the biological comes into its fulfilment in relation to the development of a fully human life. Such a shift can be spoken of in relation to a number of areas of one's life, but centrally here it involves the added capacity for a 'beloved' in addition to the earlier 'my boy or girl'. It is the child on the way to adulthood in his or her capacity to hear a call from outside the family to become one with another and thus create a new community wherein one is remade in the nexus of a form of love heretofore unknown. The failure to acquire this gift of the spirit to love another condemns many of us to an endless search at the level of biological encounter for what can be achieved only in the fullness of the spiritual relation of male and female in marriage.

What is at issue here, in my view, is not the precise accuracy of Rosenstock-Huessy's delineation of the twelve tones of the spirit or the particular names he gives to each tone. What is crucial, however, is the recognition that human unfolding is a spiritual journey.[16] Human beings are not merely chemical complexes, or adaptive animals, or socialised possibilities, but creatures whose lives move towards their fullness when they recognise and acknowledge themselves the spiritual dimensions and dynamics of their being. For Rosenstock-Huessy, 'the learning of speech'[17] is the way the Spirit enters into the human drama and invites us to live from the End back to the Present, from

16. Life is a spiritual journey and the spirit is not incidental to that journey but its very foundation. See, for example, the following study which makes an analogous point in relation to human sexuality, Herbert Richardson, *Nun, Witch, and Playmate, the Americanization of Sex*, New York: Harper & Row, 1971.

17. Rosenstock-Huessy, "Twelve Tones . . . ," p. 73.

death into life. In ways analogous to the *Spiritual Exercises* of St. Ignatius — and in the secularised gospel of Heideggerian existentialism — it is the recognition of death that is the birth of the spirit, for the spirit is the freedom to become in response to the callings laid upon our souls.[18] In Rosenstock-Huessy, 'spirit and love are stronger than death,'[19] but they are present to the human person as 'tones of the spirit' mediated in and through vital speech as the body or house of the spirit. This interior correlation is clear when one looks at the stages that precede testator: listener or obeyer, reader or conceiver, learner or wanderer, player or singer, etc., where each stage is linked to speech, spoken or written, as that which calls each stage or phase of life forward.[20]

The connection between life and death, between the spirit and the body, is reflected in Rosenstock-Huessy's 'first spiritual command,' which is 'leave a will, endow, bequeath.' By making this the first spiritual command, death is overcome, not, obviously, in the biological sense, but in the spiritual sense that the end is not extinction but a gift to subsequent generations, the resounding of one's life beyond one's death in the flow of generations. In Ignatius' *Spiritual Exercises*, we are counselled to live every moment under the horizon of the Last Judgement and to make our decisions wise by considering them under the horizon of death. As Ignatius says,

> The third rule is to consider that if I were at the point of death, what form and procedure I would wish to have observed in making this present choice. Guiding myself

18. See James Durlinger (ed.), *Ultimate Reality and Spiritual Discipline*, New York: Paragon House, 1984, which explores similar issues in a cross-traditional context.
19. Rosenstock-Huessy, "Twelve Tones . . . ," p. 69.
20. *Ibid.*, p. 73.

> by this consideration, I will make my decision on the whole matter.[21]

Such a procedure heightens one's sense of living in the present and gives to the present a depth or fullness that it lacks if each day is considered just another day. Such kinds of spiritual advice fill the spiritual literature of Christianity, but this should come as no surprise since, as Rosenstock-Huessy continually claimed, this is the secret of the Christian faith: death precedes life. But here death is not merely biological, but the daily, weekly, yearly process of letting go, abandoning dead ends, forsaking old patterns, resisting fads, etc., etc.: all those features of our lives that arise in us and block our becoming fully human. Christianity calls this 'dying to the self;' Buddhism speaks of overcoming the 'craving self' and the notion of a 'permanent self;' Hinduism calls for the overcoming of the 'ego self' in the name of the Self.[22] Indeed, the process of spiritual dying and living are deeply intertwined in Rosenstock-Huessy's vision, just as the spiritual journey of a life is intensely personal. But the point is, it seems to me, that the spirit within must be appropriated aright, for "we cannot become loquent unless we enact the words spoken to us existentially."[23]

For Rosenstock-Huessy, that human journey is an **enactment**, a living out in daily life of the twelve tones of the spirit. I recall with some vividness my first encounter with this essay more than twenty years ago when my eldest son was only three or four.

---

21. Ignatius of Loyola, *Spiritual Exercises*, Garden City, NJ: Doubleday Image, 1964, p. 86. See also the intriguing interpretation of this text by Antonio T. De Nicolas, *Powers of Imagining: Ignatius De Loyola*, New York: State University of New York Press, 1986.

22. A comparative spiritual anthropology is much needed, one that would disclose the parallels in the respective wisdom concerning humanity found in the world's religions.

23. Rosenstock-Huessy, "Twelve Tones . . . ," p. 76.

I remember sharing something of my excitement and puzzlement with a friend who also had a couple of young children. But when I remarked that Rosenstock-Huessy had identified the first tone of the spirit in the child's life was 'obey,' she immediately replied, "Boy, that shows it. He's just a typical German." Given the new-left-counter-culture in which I then moved, her response was quite predictable but still distressing. For I had also become aware that the unfolding of young lives involved something more than, as Rosenstock-Huessy expressed it, allowing young children to 'pull' themselves 'up by (their) own bootstraps. . . .'[24] In those circles there was too much of a sense that children were simply rules unto themselves rather than the newest generation in a chain of generations that stretches from creation to consummation. It is important to recognise that the tone of 'listener' is as important as that of 'obeyer.' The young must learn, respond and interact with a larger community, beginning in the family, and to heed vital speech. This is the point rather than an authoritarian order to obey.

But let me return to the point: the journey of a life, within the context of generations, is an enactment, an embodiment in that mysterious body/soul/spirit complex that we are as creatures. And it is in the very process of **living itself** that we are called by the Spirit to enact what is necessary for our full becoming. We either become the 'listener or obeyer' as a child, along with those later phases of "reader or conceiver, learner or wanderer, player or singer," or we will be crippled inwardly as adults when we will be called to be 'doubters, critics, protesters and sufferers' and thus be unable to fulfil our destinies as 'leaders teachers, prophets, and testators.'[25] Personally, I do not think that these are always the right terms, nor that his twelve tones are exhaustive, but I am very much persuaded of the truth that Rosenstock-Huessy points us towards: that at every point in the

24. Rosenstock-Huessy, "Twelve Tones . . . ," p. 73.

25. *Ibid.*, p. 73.

unfolding of our bodily life, we are met by a 'tone of the Spirit' that is essential for our full becoming. For living one's life in this way, one can become "he who experiences his dying day as a fulfilment" and thus be 'blessed.'[26]

Thus in Rosenstock-Huessy's 'Twelve Tones of the Spirit,' we encounter an example of his grammar of the spirit, an attempt to track the spirit in relation to the human journey in the context of generations. On this journey we meet the Spirit that lifts our bodily selves beyond their biological ruts and into the pathways of the spirit. Rosenstock-Huessy's awareness of the three-fold stages of that life, from childhood to adulthood to elderhood, is a crucial antidote to our monotoned Western culture that celebrates youth (remember: I am part of that generation that shouted 'never trust anyone over thirty') as consumer, producer, symbol of vitality and sexual prowess, in a technologised culture that knows only the immediacy of 'the right technique.' In a monotoned culture, we fail to allow our children to 'play before God' and our elders to 'endow and bestow.' And even we adults fail to become 'fighters for God' but instead squander our lives in petty squabbles for professional status and domination and power.[27] Outwardly, we lionise the person who has 'made it' while we inwardly cry for a sense of fulfilment. And in our desperate search for fulfilment, we mistakenly assume that it lies in things rather than in the Spirit which alone can redeem our emptiness, alone can fulfil our longing.

However, it is crucial to recognise that the Spirit that Rosenstock-Huessy calls us to recognise is present to **every phase of the human journey**. Thus in pursuit of that Spirit, we are called not to a place apart, but to our very own lives, in all their particularity and concreteness, as the place where the

26. Rosenstock-Huessy, "Twelve Tones . . . ," p. 72.

27. *Ibid.*, p. 75.

Spirit beckons. There, in your life and mine, we must find the words that truly illumine that very process of creation that 'is taking place under our very noses.' For we are the ones being created. And it is each of us, simultaneously alone yet one with humankind, that must hear aright the voice of the living Spirit that is seeking to usher us 'into our times and places, into our future destiny.'[28]

Earlier, I indicated that Rosenstock-Huessy's tracking of the Spirit was predicated on his conviction that 'spirit and love are stronger than death.' But the rest of his conviction must be acknowledged too, for he continues as follows:

> Hence, we cannot do without [spirit and love] unless we condemn ourselves to sterile futility. For to love means to become fruitful, and to be inspired means to overcome and to limit death. When the body dies, the spirit remains. The spirit proves itself to be divine whenever the trails blazed by creative, lovable lives are travelled by deliberate successors, heirs, pupils, followers, or when devilish trails are renounced and abandoned by warning posts: No trespassing!
>
> Hence, the ultimate test of the spirit is the heritage of newly acquired faculties which future generations gratefully receive and accept. . . . We had predecessors who have endowed us with acquired faculties, acquired by them and bestowed on us if we only respond by accepting them.[29]

The belief that the spirit blazes trails that we who come after can acquire is crucial because it points to the historic and enduring capacity of the living traditions of the spiritual life, of those Buddhist, Confucian, Christian, Hindu, Muslim, Sikh, Taoist,

---

28. Rosenstock-Huessy, "Twelve Tones . . . ," p. 70.
29. *Ibid.*, p. 69.

Jain, etc., pathways as the heritage of subsequent generations. These achievements of lives lived fully in the Spirit Rosenstock-Huessy here calls 'acquired faculties.' These acquired faculties, or pathways of the Spirit, are bequeathed to us in time, thus demonstrating that Chronos is not King, nor are His children simply devoured. Rather, as the offspring of the Living God, they become permanent gifts to the human race. It is, in part, this dimension of the Spirit that Rosenstock-Huessy tracks in his history, for it is history that is our temporal context and the place where the overlap of the personal and collective journeys occurs. Thus our living out of the twelve tones of the Spirit is woven into the garment of humankind's journey towards its destiny: a journey that is embodied in the story of humankind just as it is in the story of a life.

Let us now turn our attention to that larger historical drama and narrative where this process of creation is taking place in the revolutions that have given rise to nations as the nurseries for the creation of certain human types. For just as the intergenerational life journey embodies different phases, so the story of history is differentiated into the many branches of the tree that is humankind.

III

Earlier I suggested that we might see in Rosenstock-Huessy an attempt to track the spirit in the intergenerational life of humankind, in history, and in religion and culture. Here, then, I want to turn our attention to history, the story of humankind on its journey to the Ultimate. However, we should understand that this turn is not separate from what we have already examined in his 'Twelve Tones of the Spirit,' but rather adds another level to the whole story. However, at the historical level, the process of creation that Rosenstock-Huessy tracked was related to the making of peoples or nations, especially those of the West. At the heart of that process is the calling into being of 'new human types,' which, according to Rosenstock-Huessy, are not the product of the past, but a response to the call of the future, or our movement historically towards the common destiny of humankind. That end is not to be understood as static but as a dynamic process unfolding in the divinely-human story of historical creation.

John Dunne, the noted Catholic theologian from Notre Dame, distinguishes in his *A Search for God in Time and Memory* three types of consciousness in relation to time. He calls them 'the immediate, the existential, and the historic.' According to Dunne, immediate consciousness is 'restricted in awareness and concern to the here and now,' whereas existential consciousness is expanded to one's personal 'past and future.' The distinguishing feature of historical consciousness is, according to Dunne, that it extends 'beyond the confines' of one's personal lifetime 'to the past and future of mankind.'[30] These categories have a limited relevance to Rosenstock-Huessy, for in him we can see an historic consciousness at work but one that is simultaneously existential. This is clear from the very title of his great historic work *Out of Revolution: Autobiography of Western Man*, where the story of Western history is at the same time our story. His historic exploration was not for its own sake, nor for the recounting of the facts of the past, nor even to contribute to a better historiography. Rather, it was for the sake of giving voice to the divinely grounded, or better, destined, story of humankind's making as *our* story. In his own words, "the world's history is our own history."[31] Thus our making is one with the making of humankind and that making spans the future and the

---

30. See John Dunne, *A Search for God in Time and Memory*, New York: Macmillan Co., 1967, p. 211. Please excuse the term 'mankind,' but the text in question is from 1967 and thus before the feminist objections to this expression were widely heeded.

31. Eugen Rosenstock-Huessy, *Out of Revolution, Autobiography of Western Man*, p. 7.

past as the context of our present. Again, that story must be read from the end back in order that we might hear the call of our common destiny as the inner story to be heeded amidst all the twistings and turnings of events in time. As Rosenstock-Huessy remarks:

> . . . the Revolutions we have studied oblige us to insert them as stages in the natural creation of mankind. Such Revolutions carry on the process of creation. Thus political history ceases to be outside nature: man and the other forms of creation are closely akin, with the great difference that man was not created a hundred thousand years ago, but is being made before our eyes.[32]

Here the same theme of creation is invoked, but now not under our noses, but before our eyes. In history, 'before our eyes' we can see, if we have the eyes to see, the process of creation of national types, the types which are the recipients of those 'acquired faculties' we spoke of earlier. As nations are formed, they become 'nurseries' for the reproduction of those 'national types' that have been created in history through the revolutions. And these *types* then become the pathways to what we can become as the inheritors of the achievements of the past that live into the present. As Bruce Boston remarks in his study of Rosenstock-Huessy, "The human journey through history is dotted with the emergence of these new types: soldier, family member, priest, layman, king, citizen, bourgeois and proletarian."[33] And each of these types embodies a newly acquired faculty that we, in our intergenerational life, can incorporate into our lives.

More importantly, in this context we need to see the role of the religious traditions in this process of the making of humanity.

---

32. Eugen Rosenstock-Huessy, *I am an Impure Thinker*, p. 164.
33. See Bruce Boston, "'I Respond Although I Will Be Changed: The Life and Historical Thought of Eugen Rosenstock-Huessy," Ph.D. Dissertation, Princeton University, 1973, p. 308.

For it is especially here that we see the emergence of the spiritual types that have been the gift of the great religious traditions to the life and journey of humanity in relation not only to its historic ends, but also in relation to the Ultimate.

If we ask Rosenstock-Huessy what is happening in history, this is his answer:

> In history creation is going on all the time, and eternal recurrence of the created kinds is also going on all the time. The creative act that sets free new potentialities of mankind is properly called revolution. Not that creation is limited to revolutions; but in the course of history, the branches of the tree of mankind are truly regenerated — aye, by grafting they are really reproduced and changed, and this can only be done by a reconstruction of the great nurseries of men which we call nations.
>
> Revolutions do not create man; they build nurseries, as we have said before, for his reproduction in a certain way and according to a certain type.[34]

Here we see a number of crucial elements in Rosenstock-Huessy's vision. First, the central task of historical life is the reproduction of humankind itself, but **in a differentiated way**. Thus we are not all called to be the same, but different in relation to the historical task of the nation in whose nursery we happen to be born. Second, the task of the nation is the nurturing of particular types: the German prince, the English gentleman, the French citizen, the Russian proletariat. But each of these types is also exported, becoming the common heritage of humankind in relation to the different stages of the human life-cycle and phases of the spirit. Third, the creation of types in history is itself a raid upon the spiritual order of 'angels and devils' or a response to that call from beyond which elicits new powers in the human

34. Rosenstock-Huessy, *Out of Revolution*, pp. 466-7.

soul. Thus a nation's religion is, Rosenstock-Huessy notes, in relation to its time, in the 'open, between fear and faith, hate and love,' for it is in such a situation that one can pave the way to 'a new love, a new faith, a new governing power.'[35] What Rosenstock-Huessy points to here is the way newly **acquired powers** are gained in history, **acquired powers** that then are nurtured in particular national nurseries and across the body of humankind. Fourth, for Rosenstock-Huessy these new types are not fixed — "is it not intolerable for any human being to feel himself condemned once and for all, by the mere accident of birth to a fixed character?"[36] — to a certain geographical territory, but become part of the common reproductive capacities of the Spirit in time. And fifth, the creation of new types is precisely what allows the old types to also persist. The story is not, then, one of all being at the same place, but of each following its own destiny as its contribution to the whole. As Rosenstock-Huessy put it:

> The great European family of nations was not concerned with the production or fostering of ideals or material things, but with the reproduction types of the everlasting man, such as daughter, son, father, sister, mother and, of course, their combinations.[37]

But — and this is the crucial point — these types are not merely names for biological relationships, but of that constellation of acquired faculties that have been created 'before our very eyes.'

In his great work *Out of Revolution*, Rosenstock-Huessy was deeply aware of the interrelatedness of the human life-cycle and the story of revolution. As he remarks,

> the pedigree of revolutions shows that each tried to realise one neglected or imperilled potentiality of the

---

35. Rosenstock-Huessy, *Out of Revolution*, p. 474.

36. *Ibid.*

37. *Ibid.*, p. 475.

> life-cycle, and stressed its importance by establishing one great national institution to take care of the reproduction of these special processes and types. Each revolution started permanent cultural processes to mold a specific character out of plastic humanity. . . . only those revolutions are successful and memorable which obeyed the deepest need of the life-cycle.[38]

Thus the story of revolution is for Rosenstock-Huessy not primarily a story of shifting parties and persons in power, or simply of the emergence of new classes, but it is, in the midst of these, the story of humankind's response to the call from Beyond which has at its purpose 'the making of humankind.' This story is not completed in the writings of Rosenstock-Huessy: he focused on the European segment of the drama, and the critical question is whether or not the principles of historical unfolding he discovers here are adequate to the story of Africa, or of Asia or of Latin America. I believe that they are. And in the stories of these nations we will also uncover new types that are contributing to the making of our international humanity. We may also find pathways that are very much needed in the West to restore a fullness to life that has been lost in technological civilisation. For one of the things that Rosenstock-Huessy saw with such prescience was the fact that men and women

> . . . will no longer be satisfied to remain shut up within the limits of one nation's institutions and ways of life.[39]

This has unsettling consequences for societies — and may even lead to a loss of national identity or at least periods of deep confusion and uncertainty. But this is only the case when a nation is unable to recognise itself within the universal family of nations which is linked together in the common destiny to create the great singular: Humanity. For what Rosenstock-

38. Rosenstock-Huessy, *Out of Revolution*, p. 714.

39. *Ibid.*, p. 729.

Huessy recognised with such profundity was the interconnectedness of lives and nations in relation both to an Above (the Heavens) and a Below (the Earth) that conditioned every Middle (the Public or Social) and linked them one to another in a relationship of multiformity. The one is realised in the many.

If, as we have argued here, history is the story of the creation of national-human types nurtured in the life of national nurseries, then the central story running through the life-cycle of human beings and history is the task of human reproduction. But that task of human reproduction or as Rosenstock-Huessy calls it, *anthropurgy*, is not merely biological or natural, nor is it mechanical or automatic. It is rather one of humankind finding itself in response to the spirit that ever calls us beyond ourselves into the manifold chords of life played in the symphony of divine/human creation. In Rosenstock-Huessy's words,

> The dawn of creation is upon us, and we await our question, our specific mandate, in the silence of the beginnings of time. When we have learned to listen to the question and serve towards its solution, we have advanced to a new day. This is the way in which mankind has struggled forward, century after century, during the last two thousand years, building up a calendar of its rebirthdays as a true testimony of its faith.[40]

As the inheritors of 'the calendar of its rebirthdays,' we gain the acquired faculties that allow us to meet the challenges of our particular times in relation to the One time of all. Thus history is not simply the story of the past, but of the pathways ahead opened up by the pioneers who have discovered new loves — and thus new ways of being — in response to the specific mandates it was their destiny to receive. The way ahead is thus a going back to go ahead, a reliving in the phases of present life of those

40. Rosenstock-Huessy, *Out of Revolution*, p. 751.

raids on the end that have been brought back into the public sphere. As Rosenstock-Huessy put it,

> The future task is to lead man's life through a sequence of different phases and well-timed allegiances. No single allegiance can claim domination any longer over our whole life.[41]

Thus it is crucial that the past as the living context of the present be made available to human beings and societies as the way to life fulfilled.

IV

Thus far, then, we have sought to unfold something of Rosenstock-Huessy's grammar of the spirit in the intergenerational life of human beings and the international life of societies. Now we want to turn our attention to the third dimension of this quest for human making: religion and culture. If, as we have seen above, creation is taking place under our very noses and we can see it in history, then it is in the very processes of culture that that creation is embodied. In his analysis of revolution, Rosenstock-Huessy claims that "each revolution started permanent cultural processes to mold a specific character out of plastic humanity."[42] But those processes have emerged elsewhere as well: from our relationship to the earth, the cultivation of crops, the rotation of the seasons and, as well, from our relationship to the Beyond where we wrestle with demons and angels. Out of these multiform relationships emerge the pathways of the spirit that a culture is.

Nothing, perhaps, is so difficult to grasp as the life of a culture and its intimate connection with religion. Indeed, in the archaic world there is no distinction between one's religion and one's culture; they are two names for the same thing. As

41. Rosenstock-Huessy, *Out of Revolution*, p. 725.

42. *Ibid.*, p. 714.

anthropologists remind us, a culture is 'a people's way of life,' (C. Kluckhon) and, we might add, way *to* life. As a people's way of life, it is simultaneously hidden and manifest in the whole array of activities from raising children to producing the most sophisticated technical instruments, from drawing pictures to burying the dead, from cultivating crops to patterns of inward spiritual formation. And for the one immersed in the culture, it is simply life itself. For the outsider, it is a pattern of life noticeable only in its difference from one's own religio-culture. Thus cultures remain exceedingly elusive, especially from those who would seek to give voice to something that is woven as much in silence as in words, imaged as much in dreams as in works of art and architecture, lived as much in the hidden recesses of daily existence as in the public institutions of political and economic exchange. Thus it is understandable that so much of the study of culture focuses on the outward forms of its life, its material creations and manifestations, its art and architecture, its patterns of public power and ritual. Beneath all of these outer expressions of a culture's life lies its inner domain: the realm of the spirit, that uncharted and unfathomable realm where bodies and minds, imaginations and flesh, dance and twirl in the dance of life itself.

Thus, in another context, Paul Tillich argued that "culture was the form of religion, religion the substance of culture."[43] In this formula, the mystery of inner and outer is encountered, one we prefer here to speak of as the dance of life. But Tillich and Rosenstock-Huessy share a similar direction: towards culture as the house of the spirit. Rosenstock-Huessy rightly saw that speech and language were the key to this mystery, the embodied power (beyond the mind/body, idealistic/materialistic dichotomy) that simultaneously unites and distributes, that relates and differentiates, that orders and separates, that calls and ushers

43. Paul Tillich, *The Protestant Era*, Chicago: University of Chicago Press, 1948, especially the section on "Religion & Culture," pp. 55 ff.

in the manifold unity of a culture's life. Vital speech is, in this sense, a key to culture. But it is a key that opens the door to the secret of a culture: the making and remaking of humanity. We come to be what we are, in large measure, by virtue of those pathways to life given to us in our religion/culture.

In the nineteenth century, the discovery of the many religions and cultures of humankind gave rise to a vicious relativism that has continued to plague us down to the present day. According to that vicious form (not its milder relational form), the many religions and cultures render impossible the quest for human unity since they only disclose the absolute multiplicity of human types on this planet. But while the term 'culture' is not much present to Rosenstock-Huessy (it is, for example, absent from George Morgan's index in *Speech and Society*),[44] it is there in substance in his discussion of tribes. And it is there by implication in his awareness of the enduring contributions that tribes have made to humanity. But I'm getting away from my point, which is that 'timing' and 'multiformity' are the ways Rosenstock-Huessy incorporates the many cultures of humankind into the quest for the singular 'Man.' (His term: I prefer 'Humanity.')[45] That is to say, the many religions/cultures require one another in the same way as the many nation-nurseries require one another: to make for the fullness of humanity.

For Rosenstock-Huessy, an awareness of the many nations and of the many tribes led him to see something of what he called humanity's 'triple citizenship' in society, the earth, and the heavens. It is that **triple citizenship** which binds us together more than the particular configurations it has been the calling of particular peoples, tribes, and nations to realise in history. And, at the same time, it is our 'triple citizenship' which allows

44. See George Allen Morgan, *Speech and Society*, Gainesville, FL: University of Florida Press, 1987.

45. See Eugen Rosenstock-Huessy, *The Christian Future, Or the Modern Mind Outrun*, *en passant*.

us to recognise one another as brothers and sisters across those cultural configurations that separate us.[46]

When seen under the horizon of 'the making of humanity,' the multiple cultures become part of that polyphonic future towards which we move in Rosenstock-Huessy. As he says, "We have yet to establish Man, the great singular of humanity, in one household, over the plurality of races, classes and age groups. . . . They pose the questions that the third millennium will have to answer."[47] But on the way towards that future, it is crucial that we recognise the integrity of cultures as the ways that our humanity is shaped. It is the conspiracy of cultural processes to call forth a particular type of human being despite what may appear to be their diversity. This point has also been made by Richard Lannoy in his *The Speaking Tree, A Study of Indian Culture and Society* where, after acknowledging the many faces of Indian society, he goes on to say,

> Nevertheless, one cannot fail to be struck by the fact that the holistic social order is structured according to an intrinsic logic pertaining to itself, and it follows, therefore, that our legitimate task is to identify the links between the constituent elements.[48]

That holistic element is the culture that pervades the social structure, giving it its 'intrinsic logic' (better, 'mythos') in relation to that pre-eminent task of culture to make *men and women*. But that *making* varies in accordance with the way the encounter with the elemental is *spoken and named* in the living memory of the tribe or nation or culture or religion and *performed* in the

---

46. For a discussion of 'triple citizenship' in Rosenstock-Huessy see M.D. Bryant, "Revolution and World Pluralism," *The Ecumenist*, Ramsay, NJ, March-April, 1972, pp. 38-41.

47. See Rosenstock-Huessy, *The Christian Future*, p. 115.

48. Richard Lannoy, *The Speaking Tree, A Study of Indian Culture and Society*, London: Oxford University Press, 1971, p. xxi.

ritual that 'dresses' the encounter, making it possible for subsequent generations to carry on the life of the culture.

As we indicated earlier, speech is the key to culture because it is in speech that we see enacted the vital processes that enliven a people and give body to the life of a culture, that second nature which dresses us in the custom of a particular human type. Thus Rosenstock-Huessy remarks on the importance of 'learning to think more correctly about speech and dress,' where "in any ceremony, dress is used as the creator of a new 'spiritual,' social body for the man who wears that dress."[49] Thus ritual and ceremony are perhaps the closest that we can come to grasping something of the mystery of a religion and culture in its processes of making the human person by lifting that life beyond the earth through word (speech) and act (ritual), bestowing a 'second' power on the person while linking that person to a life that transcends. Here we need only think, as Rosenstock-Huessy often did, of marriage, that combination of words and acts that transforms longing and lust into the crucible for the whole future of the tribe; or of funerals that transform the terror of death into a living memory of a life lived in the context of generations. As Rosenstock-Huessy saw so clearly, a ritual

> . . . created as the victory over a negative aspect of life, consists of the acts and gestures, the sounds and words by which the appearance of order out of chaos, of shape out of confusion, can be re-lived each time the ritual is enacted.[50]

The emphasis falls here on 're-lived' in order to understand the enduring significance of cultural processes, as exemplified in rituals, in making men and women in the intergenerational context of society. As we re-live the processes by which a culture re-members and em-bodies its experience of the emergence of

49. Rosenstock-Huessy, *Origin of Speech*, p. 84.

50. *Ibid.*, p. 85.

'order out of chaos,' the new generations are linked to the older generations and are 'made' by having their experience permeated by words and gestures that raise that experience into the cultural body of the spirit. Again Rosenstock-Huessy makes the crucial point:

> As has rightly been said: 'Human life must be a living affirmation of the truth.' From the beginning of time speech has looked for forms to clothe a person's entire life in the truth.[51]

This effort is exemplified in the 'sacraments' of the Catholic tradition that link words and rituals to the crucial passages of a human life from birth to death and, as well, in the Hindu tradition which seeks the same. All the great traditions have generated rituals that form humanity in ways that accord with their own profound experience of life's depth dimensions, their experience of the Ultimate ground of things.

Of course every cultural whole requires a variety of types — priests, lawgivers, medicine men and women, technicians as well as sons and daughters, mothers and fathers, friends and clowns — and hence every culture contains a variety of rituals and processes to facilitate the emergence of those types that are required for the well-being of the whole society. Throughout his writings, but especially in *The Origin of Speech*, Rosenstock-Huessy spoke of those manifold grammatical and ritual processes which usher us to our places in the intergenerational life of society, history, and culture. But in every case, this ushering took place through the medium of speech which 'was established to call forth life.'[52] When we follow his lead, we can then begin to penetrate the life of a culture and see something of the dynamic that lies at its heart. That dynamic is the making of men and women in the nexus of speech and ritual. For speech and ritual

---

51. Rosenstock-Huessy, *Origin of Speech*, p. 96.

52. *Ibid.*, p. 45.

(which are not limited to formal acts but are present as informal pathways of interaction as well) are the carriers of the spirit that lift life beyond the merely biological, lift experience beyond mere happening, and lift the mind beyond mere mental activity into a level of vitality, meaning and orientation wherein we may come to the fullness of our humanity by, in Rosenstock-Huessy's words, being "threaded into God's creation, day after day."[53] That creation is, as we have seen, being enacted under our very noses in the 'twelve tones of the spirit,' it is there to be seen in history where human types are called into being, is being lived in the very cultural processes which make a culture a living aquired nature, and in the religious traditions which remake us in the spiritual types that link us to the Ultimate. All of these are making us what we are becoming and fitting us for the polyphonic dance of humanity in the presence of the divine.

This whole spiritual process has been obscured for those of us who live in a technological civilisation obsessed by the making of things to consume and destroy, rather than the making of human beings in their wonderful interdependent variety and multiformity. Can we recover the hidden life of the spirit that enlivens that life-cycle, emblazons history, and embodies culture? Can we remember what 'has been forgotten in secularism?'[54] Can we relearn what has been lost in the changing fads of our educators? For Rosenstock-Huessy, one of the secrets of humankind is hidden in the syllable 're.' For it is precisely the power of human beings to 're'-make life. Not of course in the dangerously distorted nightmare that seems to have captivated our biological scientists, but in the fully human sense that we remain forever capable of response, of heeding that call of the spirit that is the crucible of all our making and remaking.[55]

---

53. Rosenstock-Huessy, *Origin of Speech*, p. 71.

54. *Ibid.*, p. 73.

55. *Ibid.*, pp. 734ff

V

In this chapter, then, we have sought to unfold something of Rosenstock-Huessy's grammar of the spirit in the making of a polyphonic humanity. Beginning with his "Twelve Tones of the Spirit", we were led to see the presence of the spirit in relation to the twelve phases of life that span the life of human beings in the stages of childhood, adulthood, and elderhood. Here we saw something of the way the spirit brings to fulfilment a phase of a life by calling forth that which is necessary to the unfolding of a fully human life. These processes were, we saw, intergenerational and thus social. Human life thus becomes human through the enactment of acquired faculties, faculties that are the gift of pioneers in the past who give them as gifts of the spirit to subsequent generations. Thus the spirit and love prove stronger than death by leaping over death to inspire the next generation, calling it to transcend, to go beyond the merely given in the life-cycle to appropriate the **acquired** gifts of the spirit in the order of time.

Consequently, we turned our attention to history where we can see the making of humankind unfolding in the great revolutions that have permeated Western historical life. We acknowledged that this analysis must be extended to the non-Western nations. Out of the revolutions nation-nurseries were formed that nurtured distinct human types. But these types — for example, those of gentleman and citizen — were not confined to one nation, but spread to others as well. Thus we can see something of the inter-dependent character of the making of nations, but, more importantly, we can see the role of revolutions and nations in the calling into being of certain human types which are for the sake of the whole of humankind. This, too, is a tracking of the Spirit in the process of anthropurgy or 'the making of man.' And finally, we turned to the processes of culture and religion, especially speech and ritual, to see something of the meaning of becoming human. We saw something of the interface of religion and culture in this process. The point was that our 'plastic humanity' is addressed in word and act, and in our responses within a culture and a religion, we become human in the distinctive dress of a particular culture and the spiritual type of a given tradition of religious life. Such a becoming is not separate from the great Singular that is humankind, but rather the tone we enact in the great symphony: the making of humankind.[56]

Throughout, we have focused on the Spirit in that drama of 'man-making' not in order to mystify the process, but in order to recover what has been lost in the midst of the consumerism, materialism, and secularism that is too much with us. Moreover, the spirit stands as an antidote to a technological self-sufficiency which has forgotten that we are made in response to Transcendence which calls us from Beyond to transcend and to discover ourselves in relation to the Ultimate ground and end of life. It is as we hear that call and respond that we are made, unmade and remade in the forge of a Love, to use the language of Christianity, that calls from the End back into the Present of each life at each moment. It is the call that concludes the last stanza of W.H. Auden's *Aubade*, a poem written in memory of Rosenstock-Huessy:

> But time, the Domain of Deeds,
> calls for a complex Grammar
> with many Moods and Tenses,
> and prime the Imperative.
> We are free to choose our paths,
> but choose We must, no matter
> where they lead, and the tales
> we tell of the past must be true.

---

56. Though derived from Rosenstock-Huessy, we have sought to make it our own and extend it here.

Human Time is a City
where each inhabitant has
a political duty nobody else can perform,
made cogent by her Motto:
LISTEN MORTALS, LEST WE DIE![57]

Here Auden recognises the remarkable grammar of the spirit that we find in the writings of Eugen Rosenstock-Huessy, a grammar that enables us to respond to the call of the Spirit that seeks to see life fulfilled in its relation to the Ultimate.

---

57. This W.H. Auden poem appeared in *The New Yorker* within the year after Rosenstock-Huessy's death in 1973.

5

Woven on the Loom of Time

In this concluding lecture, it remains for me only to summarise the major themes of my presentation and to offer a synoptic account of my thesis. These lectures have attempted a number of things in response to the subject of the Miller Lectures, "the one unfolding purpose through the ages," a purpose that must, we have argued, take into account the multiform religious traditions of humankind. I have argued that that purpose, witnessed to in diverse ways, is the making of humanity in relation to the Ultimate.

In the opening lecture, I outlined some of the modern challenges to the subject of the Miller Lectures. Central here is the view that the whole of reality is reducible to the world known in the empirical sciences or scientism. But I also acknowledged that one cannot simply assume the universality of Christian modes of discourse in addressing our subject. Instead, I outlined seven assumptions that marked these lectures, assumptions that constitute my dissent from the characteristic pretense of modernity, namely, that *God is an unnecessary hypothesis.* Against this pretense I sought to ground this exposition in the assumption that (i) the religious traditions are the source of wisdom on life's deepest questions and that, in our post-modern situation, (ii) one must seek that wisdom not in one tradition as opposed to another, but across traditions.[1] This does not, however,

1. This is an essential point. It has now become an academic →

entail syncretism, but simply an expectation that truth is not limited to one tradition but will find confirmation, though in its own distinctive discourse, in the wisdom of other, if not all, traditions.

Moreover, these lectures assume, as the reader is now well aware, that (iii) history is the story of humanity's encounter with transcendence, that it is an unfolding within the dialectic of time and eternity.[2] Thus in turning to the religious traditions of humankind — and not just to my own Christian tradition — I attempt (iv) to pay attention to the *mythic narratives* of humankind and (v) to read those traditions in terms of the way in which they provide a living orientation to life that clothes the adherent in a distinctive human faith. Though I acknowledge with gratitude my own Christian orientation, I also seek (vi) to see the destiny of humankind in more than Christian terms and (vii) to acknowledge that meaning and purpose are not static but unfold in the very quest for the Absolute that is central to humanity.

These assumptions, then, led me to four affirmations. The

→ common place to argue that all our thinking is formed by our particular traditions and thus cannot claim universality. There is often a confusion here. We should all be grateful for the wisdom that is given to us in our particular traditions, but that wisdom always exceeds the tradition itself. And in leading us beyond, we are led to the truth given in that wisdom. The confusion lies in mistaking the container for the product, in identifying the truth with the language in which it is expressed. The universality of truth lies not in the formulation but in that insight or wisdom that we achieve. On the other hand, it is essential that we not limit the truth to the form of its formulation in a given tradition. It is this dialectic that I hope I respect here.

2. An impressive text relevant to our theme of time and eternity that I did not encounter until after I had given the Miller Lectures is Robert Neville, *Eternity and Time's Flow*, Albany, NY: SUNY Press, 1993. It is an outstanding study and if I had encountered it earlier it would have altered my articulation of these matters at this point.

first affirmation signaled my dissent from a modernity that would affirm that the deepest human purpose is in relation to any material having. Instead, I affirm (i) that humanity achieves its deepest purpose only in relation to the Ultimate. This is no new affirmation, but simply a reaffirmation of what, as far as I can see, the great traditions of religious life have always taught — even when they failed to live it. The gloss that I attempt to develop is that that purpose is, in part, fulfilled through the variety of humankind's religious traditions. In such a view, the achievement of a single purpose requires the diversity of traditions in order that the fullness of that purpose be accomplished.

This affirmation that humanity is to be related to the Ultimate is not, as some would allege, an empty affirmation that leads to disenchantment with the world or a withdrawal from the everyday. Rather, both the world and the everyday come into a new perspective as they come into view as the gifted setting of life and the context of realising our proper ends as human beings. But to be attached to them, to confuse the mundane with the absolute is a perennial human confusion that distorts our proper relation to the world and the everyday. When we elevate the finite to the status of the infinite, or identify the spiritual with the material, or confuse our being with our having, then we lose, as the great traditions of spiritual life realise, our proper direction and orientation towards the Ultimate. But to see this Ultimate purpose aright is to (ii) see history as the spiritual story of human unfolding towards its proper destiny in God. The language of the Ultimate is always problematic given the diversity of humanity's religious pathways; but the truth that the centre of the human story is neither power nor consumption, but transcends the mundane in the life of the spirit, is a common witness shared across tradition.

This common witness of the religious traditions to a purpose beyond the mundane (iii) discloses the heart of the human story as the making of humanity in relation to the Ultimate. Such a purpose is realised in the manifold traditions of human religious life which clothe and shape that quest for the Ultimate. Humanity is thus formed in the image of the Ultimate that has been given in the particular configurations in the multiform traditions of religious life. Such a view of religion does not deny the historical ambiguities of the religious traditions but does affirm their inner heart as conformity to the divine. Thus (iv) the harmony of the great religious traditions does not lie in any identity of doctrine, rite, or practice — on this level plurality, diversity, difference is the order of the day — but in the *telos* of religion — in that which always exceeds them, the Ultimate itself. These assumptions and affirmations inform the exploration that is unfolded in the lectures themselves.

Although I find myself inspired and persuaded by the classical formulations of the great religious traditions, I acknowledge that for many in the modern age the wisdom of the great religious traditions has become hidden. Thus in the second lecture on 'dialogical humanity,' I offered a contemporary argument that seeks to ground the human in its dialogue with Transcendence or the Ultimate. The eclipse of transcendence in the world-view of modernity is, I believe, a profound mistake. For the loss of God is simultaneously and necessarily the loss of humanity. In the language of the classical Christian tradition, we could say that the eclipse of transcendence is simultaneously the eclipse of the created dignity of humanity. Or, in the language of classical Mahāyāna Buddhism, we could say that the eclipse of transcendence leads to a failure to acknowledge the *buddha-nature* that is the heart of humanity. My argument, however, was not pursued in these classical discourses of the religious traditions, but through the introduction of the thought of two twentieth-century thinkers, Martin Buber and Eugen Rosenstock-Huessy. In concert with their insights, I sought to make the case that transcendence is not peripheral to humanity, nor is it accidental. Rather, I claim, along with Buber and Rosenstock-Huessy, that it is constitutive of humanity.

Transcendence is not, however, primarily an object of thought, but it is a living Presence at the very heart of humanity. Thus the human is constituted by its dialogical relation with the divine in its four-foldedness in time and space.

It is, I continued, in the relatedness of humanity that we discover our dialogical humanity that links us simultaneously in the world of space and time and yet transcends that world. In this existential and philosopical perspective, then, I think we can see more clearly how the religious traditions are 'dialogues with Transcendence.' It was the intention of the second lecture to make more intelligible the conviction that humanity is constituted by the Ultimate and unfolds in dialogue with Transcendence. This is, as I indicated before, a classical affirmation of the great religious traditions. But it was presented here in more contemporary idiom in an effort to address those unable to hear the discourse of the great traditions. I left unaddressed in that lecture the other dimension of the triadic matrix of human destiny, namely, the earth.[3] But that will have

---

3. Concern with the earth has emerged as a crucial issue in much of my recent research. In large part, this has grown out of a local environmental issue, namely, the closure of the water supply in 1989 in the town of Elmira, where I live, due to the chemical pollution of our water by Uniroyal Chemical, a multinational corporation headquartered in the USA. Since that time, a group of local citizens has been engaged in attempting to require Uniroyal to contain the site and clean up the polluted aquifers. My first contribution was "Notes Towards an Eco-Spirituality, Recovering a Living Planet" for a New ERA conference in 1990 on the theme of 'Healing the Earth.' I have also contributed as article on "God, Humanity, & Mother Earth: African Wisdom and the Recovery of the Earth," pp. 69-80, in Gilbert Ogutu (ed.), *God, Humanity and Mother Nature*, Nairobi: Masaki Publishers, 1992; "Ecological Responsibility and Interfaith Dialogue," in *Tibet House Bulletin*, Spring 1994, pp. 1-5; and "Ecological Evil and Caring for the Earth" in a forthcoming volume on *The Reality of Evil, Responses of the World Religions*, ed. by Willian Cenkner.

to remain for another occasion. I concluded this lecture with some remarks on interreligious encounter and dialogue as an important contemporary development wherein we might come to recognise our common but multiform religious pilgrimage towards our destiny in God.

In the third lecture, I turned to the great religious traditions and offered sketches of several traditions in an effort to point to the divine-human type that each tradition contributes to the process of making humanity in relation to the Ultimate. In this perspective, the multiform religious traditions are perceived not as rivals but as collaborators in the historical task of the making of humanity in relation to the Ultimate. Each has contributed a spiritual type that is integral to the fullness of polyphonic humanity in relation to the destiny of humanity in the Ultimate. Thus our shared destiny to be related to the Ultimate is realised, in part, through the multiform religious Ways that have emerged in time as the dialogical revelation given to humanity in the crucible of Transcendence.

In my presentation of six of the Ways to the Ultimate given in the historic life of humanity, I attempted to allow the traditions to speak in their own distinctive tongues. Thus I do not equate the Hindu quest for *mokṣa* with the Christian quest for *Salvation* or the Buddhist quest for *Enlightenment*. There is, of course, a structural parallel here, but the multiform substantive ways of speaking of the spiritual end sought in each tradition is affirmed. This multiformity is necessary to the completeness of the whole, namely, the human family realised in the Ultimate.

Thus we sought to see the Hindu Way as a Way that incorporates diversity within itself according to its own recognition of the diverse dominances within the human self—the affective, the reflective/intuitive, the active, and the experiential. In the swirl of Hindu religious life, the Dancing Divine entrances our ignorant selves to find ourselves in the Absolute playing at the heart of all. This Dharmic Way shapes humanity in conformity to its fundamental experiences of divine reality and gives us the Hindu as a distinctive spiritual type within the human family. The paths to liberation or *mokṣa* of humanity from *saṁsāra* give us the gift of the Hindu in the making of humanity.

The Buddhist Way addresses itself to the issue of *duḥkha* or suffering. Emerging out of Siddhārtha's experience of Enlightenment, the Buddhist Way seeks to rescue humanity from its suffering through the Eight-Fold Path. While it does not preoccupy itself with speculation on the Ultimate — lest the suffering victim die awaiting the outcome of such speculation — the Buddhist Way does affirm humanity's ability to transcend or overcome suffering and realise *nirvāṇa*. The practice of the Buddha's Way has made and remade humanity as the gift of the Buddhist to the whole of humankind.

The Christian Way seeks to restore humanity to the fullness of its unity with God through Jesus Christ. Broken by sin, humankind is disordered in ways that can be healed through the One who is Life, the Christ. In the Christian Way the path of restoration to communion with God goes, for many, through the sacramental church, for many others, through a personal relationship to the Risen Lord, and, for still others, through a life of discipleship. But this diversity of Christian understanding shares the central conviction that the Incarnate Word leads us to Life in God and gives to the making of humanity the Christian.

The Muslim Way emerges when Muhammad is called to 'Recite,' and receives the gift of the *Korān*. And as the gift is 'Recited,' humanity is recalled from its forgetfulness to Allāh, its divine creator. The Muslim Way unfolds through the 'Five Pillars' which include the ringing affirmation to all humanity that "There is no God but God and Muhammad is His Prophet." The Muslim Way extends the Divine Will to the whole of humanity's life in time and thus creates Muslims, those who submit and find peace.

Master Kung or Confucius is the historical heart of the Confucian Way even though he claims simply to transmit ancient wisdom. It is Confucius who gave humanity a teaching on the Five Human Relationships — husband/wife, father/son, elder brother/junior brother, elder friend/junior friend, ruler/subject — that served to create social bonds of unity for countless generations. Moreover, his insight into *Jen*, or human-heartedness, shaped humanity in ways that gave to the world the Confucian. Similarly, when Guru Nānak heard the call of God to be 'God's minstrel' to sing God's praises, he learned a Way that led others as well to the Divine Guru. And he thus gave to humanity the ecstatic disciple, the Sikh.

Thus the encounter with the Divine in each tradition resulted in a symphony of Ways that have served to recreate humanity in accord with their distinctive dialogue with the Ultimate. While each of these dialogues with Transcendence is addressed to humanity as such, it is only some within the human family who have heard and responded. And in their response they are realising the gift to the whole of humanity given in their particular way to the Ultimate. Thus it is polyphonic humanity, humanity in its glorious multiformity, that witnesses to the glory on the Unmanifest Source and End of our Destiny.

In the fourth lecture, I shifted ground again in an effort to provide a more detailed examination of a particular grammar of the spirit. Again, I turned to the work of Eugen Rosenstock-Huessy for guidance and outlined his attempt to track the life of the spirit in the personal, intergenerational, and historical life of humankind. Though this account reflects its Christian inspiration it is open to correction by the wisdom of other traditions. The merit of his view is that the spirit is acknowledged not as the left-over dimension of humanity but as the vital and dynamic heart of the human. Thus there is a movement towards the Ultimate, a dynamic striving for the Real present to the whole of life.

Rosenstock-Huessy's grammar uncovers the spirit in the '12 tones of the spirit' that pervade personal and intergenerational life and give it its dynamic and wholeness. As we live through the stages of life as children, adults, and elders, we are called to unfold the spirit in ways that link life across generations. Thus the human journey itself is an enactment and unfolding which shows that the spirit of love is stronger than death. In an analogous way, then, we hold with Rosenstock-Huessy that we can see aright the story of the making of nations when we see its deeper meaning of making nurseries for the nurturing of national types. But such nation-building is saved from idolatrous distortion and murderous chauvinism only when it is set within the context of the family of nations and the making of humanity in God. Cultures and religions are likewise central to this spiritual making of humanity in order to conform humanity to its proper End and Goal in the Ultimate.

These lectures are, then, an attempt to see the unfolding divine purposes as lifting humanity into the life of the Ultimate, a purpose unfolded in and through the great religious traditions. But our sketch is neither adequate nor complete. It is a mere finger pointing to what exceeds us. For the reality is the harmony of the Ultimate given to humanity in the religious traditions but fulfilled only Beyond. This is but a poor witness to that divine destiny which always exceeds our words and schemes but ever illumines and beckons our minds and hearts.

My attempt has been to discern a harmony amidst the cacophany of the many voices of the religious life. If, as I have argued here, we approach that cacophany with eyes turned towards the Beyond from which we come and towards which we go, then perhaps we can see something more than dissonance. If we can see the religious traditions not as contradictory conceptualities but as diverse revelatory gifts to humanity of that Ultimate Mystery, then perhaps we can glimpse something of the cosmic harmony. If we remember that the Absolute seeks to make itself known to humanity for the sake of a transforming communion rather than a clamorous competition, then perhaps we can affirm the manifold Ways to the Ultimate as a witness to that which ever exceeds. If we can relearn the primacy of the Spirit that makes us what we become, then perhaps we can move beyond the technological closure that threatens our future.

If I am right in claiming that human destiny is the making of humanity in relation to the Ultimate, then the current encounter and dialogue between religions emerges as a special locus of that purpose in our time. For it is here that we are beginning to overcome a history of religious antagonism that has been too prevalent in the story of human religious life. At the same time, we must avoid turning that encounter and dialogue into a new chapter of the modern epoch, one which denies religion as a Way to the Absolute.

We can see now the beginnings of recognition of the spiritual kinship of religions, a kinship that should lead to mutual respect and willingness to learn from the gifts of the spirit given in each religious Way. Moreover, we can begin to recognise that our sister Buddhists, Hindus, Muslims, Confucians, Sikhs, and Christians truly are our brothers and sisters in that great family of religious/spiritual types/ways that has unfolded in the midst of time in its journey towards the Ultimate. It is our hope that the discordant clash of many Ways, views and voices across the religious world can be transformed into a new symphony in praise of the harmony of the Beyond that beckons us all, while weaving us into one human family, but forever exceeds our grasp.

6

Epilogue

I

beginningless beginning
silent
eternal
dharma
ultimate
absolute
tao
mystery
glory
not being
nor non-being
not full void
nor empty fullness
not is
nor is not
beyond
all

II

everflowing
going out
creating

time-space
becoming
chronos
moving
universes within universes
unfolding
knit with love
laced with grace
eternity in time

III

spirit
life
myriad forms
from beyond
yet here
enfleshed
being and becoming
journeying
in time
through time
this a place to be
fitting
yet not our end

IV

beckoned to become
in human form
shaped by pathways of the spirit
revealed at different times
in different places
gifts of the Beyond
to searching striving hearts
open to the higher call

made know in the *ṛṣi*,
prophet, master,
christ, saint, *guru*,
buddha,
and *bodhisattva* too
pioneers of the spirit
blazing trails
that sing of life
full abundant
free

V

making wombs
where spirit thrives
gives birth
to heaven's ways
in sacred gestures
righteous acts
silence within
holy words
that make us whole
beyond
ignorance
sin
duḥkha
grasping
inpropriety
forgetfulness
manifold faces of *māyā*
blocking binding bonding
the way to the real

VI

born for bliss

awareness
being
caught in bonds
that cut deep
across the flame
dim life and light
leave sorrow
anger
disorder
ignorance
separation
and pain
where union
awareness compassion and joy
were meant to be

VII

until
the spirit
calls
awakens slumbering souls
leads us
to paths with heart
where healing grows
stage by stage
we learn the way
that leads to
one
already there
amidst our twisting
our turning in *māyā*'s lair

VIII

each is dressed

in one of *dharma*'s many forms
of humanity made whole in buddha silence
muslim recitation or confucian bows
hindu *oṁ*s or christ's cross or sikh songs
jewish commandments or native sweetgrass
history's loom
weaves out of many threads
the seamless robe
of humankind
made one
in
many

VIII

the frog in the well
knows a universe as big as his pond
his way the only way
complete in itself
fully divine
yet not exhaustive
beyond it lie
other ways
fully present too
to sun's rays
to light's radiance
we honour them
place them in the whole.

IX

come home
to joy
find peace
within
vanquish fear

do good
let love reign
let compassion grow
until we know
where we belong
union divine
communion restored
not mine or thine
but many become one
harmony
of the great singular
won

Glossary

ānanda: bliss, joy.

anatta: no self, or not self. In Buddhism, the doctrine of *anatta* affirms that there is no "fixed permanent self;" self is to be overcome.

ātman: the deeper Self, one's inmost Self, the Self that is one with *Brahman* in many Hindu traditions.

avatāra: a manifestation of the Absolute, Kṛṣṇa is an *avatāra* of Viṣṇu.

Bhagavad Gītā: "The Song of God" is part of the great Hindu epic, *Mahābhārata*. It was the favourite sacred text of Mahatma Gandhi. It is the most well-known "sacred literature" of the Hindu tradition.

bhaktas: a devotee, one who practices devotion to their lord.

bhakti-yoga: the *yoga*/way of devotion, a pathway to the divine.

brahman/*Braham*: the ultimate, the supreme principle of all, the Absolute.

bodhisattva: In Mahāyāna or northern Buddhism, the *bodhisattva* is one who, rather than entering *nirvāṇa*, returns to work for the enlightenment of all sentient beings. In Tibetan Buddhism, the *bodhisattva* Way is focused on the cultivation of compassion for all living beings. The most famous *bodhisattva* figure is Avalokiteśvara or Kuan-yin in China or Kannon in Japan.

cit: awareness, thought, knowledge, perception.

Dhammapada: part of the Pāli canon of Buddhist *sūtras*/scriptures. It is considered the most succint summary of the teaching of the Enlightened One, the Buddha. It is comprised of four hundred and twenty three verses.

dharma: cosmic order of all things; a particular religious Way including rites, doctrines, laws and institutions; norms of behaviour present to all things.

din: (Arabic) the closest equivalent to "religion" but having some resonance with *dharma*.

duḥkha/*dukkha*: suffering, the term *duḥkha*/*dukkha* is part of the First Noble Truth in the teachings of Buddhism: Life is *duḥkha*. This is most familiarly translated as "Life is Suffering." But Buddhist interpreters always insist that its meaning is more than suffering, that it points to the brokenness of life, that life is 'out of joint'.

guru: teacher or master, the one who leads the student from darkness to light.

jñāna-yoga: the *yoga*/way of knowledge, one of the paths to the Ultimate.

karma: action, the results of acts done in a previous life.

karma-yoga: the *yoga*/way of action, a path to the divine.

līlā: sport or play; in many Hindu traditions, creation is said to be "divine play."

Mahābhārata: along with the *Rāmāyaṇa*, the great epics of the Hindu tradition. The *Bhagavad Gītā* is found in the *Mahābhārata*.

māyā:a condition of the world, or the power of illusion that binds humanity to *saṁsāra*.

mokṣa: liberation, release, the final liberation from *saṁsāra*.

nirvāṇa: the going out of the flame of desire, in Buddhism it is often seen as the highest state, the final liberation when there will be no further rebirth.

puruṣa: the human, the ideal human.

rāja-yoga: the way/*yoga* of discipline; one path to the Ultimate.

ṛṣi: a Vedic seer, wise one.

sat: being; real, true.

sat-cit-ānanda: being-awareness (knowledge)-bliss is a formula for the Absolute.

saṁgha/saṅgha: the community, one of the Triple Jewels in Buddhism. Buddhists take refuge in the *dharma*, the *buddha*, and the *saṁgha*.

saṁsāra: the realm of the world, the cycle of rebirth, the ceaseless flux of things.

sannyāsa/sannyāsī: the life of total renunciation, one who has renounced everything, the final stage in Hindu life.

satori: the Japanese term for enlightenment, it has the connotation of sudden illumination.

tanha: craving desire, in Buddhism the second noble truth is that the cause of *duḥkha* (suffering) is *tanha* (craving desire).

yoga/yogas: a discipline that leads to union with the divine, those disciplines/ paths/ways that lead to union with the divine.

Index